7 Arrows

Transformational Prayer

for a Culture in Crisis

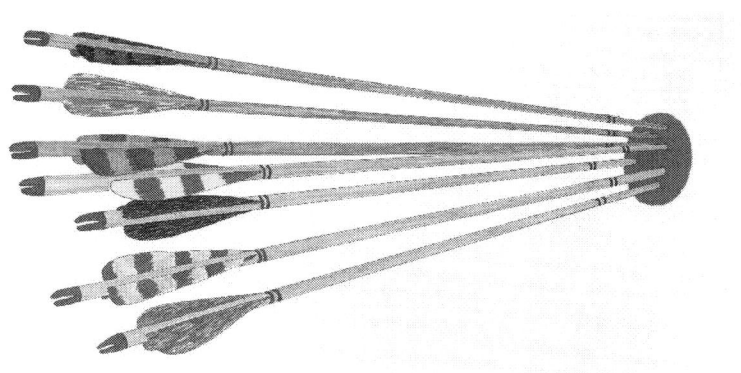

Evalyn Benton

All Scriptures are taken from the *Holy Bible, New International Version* unless otherwise noted.
Copyright © 2016 by Christian Media Bibles. Used by permission.

7 Arrows: Transformational Prayer for a Culture in Crisis
Copyright © 2020 Evalyn Benton

All rights reserved. Except as permitted under the US Copyright Act of 1976, no part of this publication may be reproduced, distributed or transmitted in any form or by any means electronic or mechanical, including photocopying, recording, or any information storage/database system and retrieval system now known or to be invented, without prior permission in writing from the author, except by a reviewer who wishes to quote brief parts of the text in connection with a review written for inclusion in a source of media.

Cover Design/Interior Design: Lindsay Fleming
Chapter Art: Chris Pfohl
Nightingale: iStock-1097778920

Printed in the United States of America
ISBN: 9781706936541
Library of Congress Control Number: 2019920275

DEDICATED WITH LOVE

To Sam, my love, you are a rock. You are our family's hero. No words can thank you enough for the example of Jesus that you are to us. Thank you for all of the love and joy you bring to us every day. Thank you for supporting my dreams.

To our children, Leah, Joseph, Ashley, Frances, Andrew, John, Taylor and our granddaughter, Bellamy, this book was written for you. You are God's most precious gifts. Your fellowship is our most treasured earthly joy. *You are deeply loved.* May you be "rooted and grounded in love and have power, together with all the saints, *to comprehend* the length and width and height and depth of His love, and to *know the love of Christ* that surpasses knowledge; may you be filled with all the fullness of God."

WITH HONOR

To these sisters in Christ whose friendship, wisdom and intercession have enriched my life beyond measure. Through suffering and trials, *many waters cannot quench love.*

To Pam Pulsfort, in heaven, my comrade in arms, the strength of my right hand, we are joined forever by our prayers. I love and miss you.

To Sharon Mitchell, heroine of the faith, thank you for your consistent prayers for me. You are my dearest friend, and I love you.

To Marilyn Howard, beautiful intercessor, governmental servant-leader and my cheerleader on this project, may we take cities together!

With Gratitude

I thank my God every time I remember you. In every prayer for all of you, I always pray with joy, because of your partnership in the gospel from the first day until now…It is right for me to feel this way about all of you, since I have you in my heart. Philippians 1:3-5, 7

Over the last few years, these family members and closest friends have carried my husband and me through the most challenging season of our lives. We are deeply grateful to Marion 'Pat' and Connie Plemmons, Darrell and Alda Burston, Jeff and Susan Hutchins for your incredible love and generosity. We carry you in our hearts.

With deepest gratitude, we also thank Clint and Rose Ann Summers, Ryan and Jane Long, the Benton children, Allan and Marilyn Howard, La Rue Groves, Will and Joyce Robinson for your friendship and support.

To Lindsay Fleming: Without your encouragement, patience and expertise, this book would not have been completed. Thank you for sharing your genius. "Those who hope in the LORD will renew their strength. They will soar on wings like eagles."

Preface

"The most effective way to destroy people is to deny and obliterate their own understanding of their history."

George Orwell

"I have one great political idea…That idea is an old one. It is widely and generally assented to; nevertheless, it is very generally trampled upon and disregarded. – The best expression of it, I have found in the Bible. It is, in substance: *Righteousness exalteth a nation- sin is a reproach to any people.* This constitutes my politics, the negative and positive of my politics, and the whole of my politics."

Frederick Douglass

The Nightingale

The nightingale is a small, common bird whose song among other birds is unique. Upon the backdrop of darkness, the nightingale sings a strong, clear melody that rises above competing noises of the night. The song of the nightingale is considered to be one of the most beautiful sounds in nature. The nightingale sings to proclaim that although there is darkness, the light of morning will surely come.

So, too, the voices of the prophets rise during times of deep darkness. With a clear, strong message, prophets of old and prophets today send forth a beautifully piercing sound.

7 Arrows is the song of the nightingale, a candle in the darkness that illuminates a path. It is a clarion call to believers - to rededicate their lives to Christ - to pray and to act in order to bring transformation to our communities and our nation.

> *Arise, shine, for your light has come, and the glory of the Lord rises upon you. See, darkness covers the earth and thick darkness is over the peoples, but the Lord rises upon you and his glory appears over you. Nations will come to your light, and kings to the brightness of your dawn.*
>
> Isaiah 60:1-3

Table of Contents

Chapter 1: Lift Your Voice 1
Chapter 2: The Call 9
Chapter 3: Days of Prayer and Fasting 21
Chapter 4: Poised for an Awakening 35
Chapter 5: Lessons in Prayer 45
Chapter 6: Seven Arrows 55
Arrow 1: Self-Government 59
Arrow 2: Family Government 75
Arrow 3: Church Government 101
Arrow 4: State and Local Governments 113
Arrow 5: The Federal Government 121
Arrow 6: News & Media 167
Arrow 7: The Preaching of the Gospel 173
Final Thoughts 187
Addendum One 189
Addendum Two 193
End Notes 197

"Come, let us return to the LORD.

Let us know, let us press on to know the LORD."

Hosea 6: 1, 3

Chapter 1: Lift Your Voice

A STUDENT OF CULTURE

Having grown up in a family and circle of friends that included state politicians, early on I became a student of government. From the time that I was a child, our family attended rallies during election cycles and discussed aspects of culture and government at family gatherings. In college, I worked in the State House in South Carolina and pursued a minor in U.S. History, while majoring in British Literature.

In 1981, I became a Christian. In 1984, I was blessed to marry Sam, a chaplain at the University of South Carolina. We have served in leadership roles in churches and as associate and senior pastors over the last thirty-five years.

I have always had a passion for truth and for the application of truth to our lives. The life stories of individuals throughout history and the rise and fall of civilizations fascinates me. As a young wife and mother, I continued my studies of culture and history by reading hundreds of biographies, histories and textbooks while I educated my four children at home. Later, while serving in Women's ministry at my church, I taught Expository Writing for nine years in the community college system in Charlotte, N.C. For the last few years, I have studied World Civilizations and U.S. History, extensively, and taught both of these courses at the secondary level.

Jesus challenges us to be aware of and to understand the times in which we live. He challenges us as he did those around him, with these words,

"When evening comes, you say, 'It will be fair weather, for the sky is red,' and in the morning, 'Today it will be stormy, for the sky is red and overcast,' indicating that the people of his day used signs and signals to interpret and predict the day's weather. He reproved them when he said, 'you know how to interpret the appearance of the sky, but you cannot interpret the signs of the times.'" Matthew 16:3

Conversely, in the Old Testament, the sons from the tribe of Issachar were praised because they "understood the times and knew what to do." 1 Chronicles 12:32 These discerning men were thoughtful enough to understand the events that occurred in their nation and were wise enough to know the actions that should be taken.

Americans now find themselves at a significant juncture in history and in a season of great need. *7 Arrows* offers an interpretation of and solutions to America's current cultural challenges. It intertwines my knowledge of government and the church with Biblical knowledge in order to find solutions. *7 Arrows* will inspire and equip you to use your voice to intercede for families, churches, cities and our nation and birth within you a desire to take an active role in bringing Biblical principles into every sphere of culture.

MY VOICE, A LIFE DEDICATED TO PRAYER

Since 1981, participation in small group prayer meetings has been a consistent and significant part of my life. My focus for prayer has been my family, church leaders and civil government. I have prayed into cultural issues and interceded for the welfare of America for almost four decades.

Through the years, I have been mentored by men and women who have a passion for Christ and who carry gifts of discernment, prophecy and intercession. During the 1990's, I had the privilege of praying each Thursday evening with two leading intercessors in the Raleigh-Durham-Chapel Hill area. God met us in our meetings with His Presence; we experienced His love and His power every week over a nine-year period.

INTIMACY WITH CHRIST

During this time, I learned many things, but two key lessons stand out. The first is from Matthew 25, verses 1-13, where Jesus contrasts the wisdom of the five believers who were prepared and ready for the appearance of Jesus with the five who grew drowsy in the night. Maintaining oil in their lanterns, the wise young women lived with purpose and focus.

Consider the words of Jesus' parable:

> *At that time the kingdom of heaven will be like ten virgins who took their lamps and went out to meet the bridegroom. Five of them were foolish and five were wise. The foolish ones took their lamps but did not take any oil with them. The wise ones, however, took oil in jars along with their lamps. The bridegroom was a long time in coming, and they all became drowsy and fell asleep. At midnight the cry rang out: "Here's the bridegroom! Come out to meet him!" Then all*

the virgins woke up and trimmed their lamps. The foolish ones said to the wise, "Give us some of your oil; our lamps are going out." "No," they replied, "there may not be enough for both us and you. Instead, go to those who sell oil and buy some for yourselves." But while they were on their way to buy the oil, the bridegroom arrived. The virgins who were ready went in with him to the wedding banquet. And the door was shut. Later the others also came. "Lord, Lord," they said, "open the door for us!" But he replied, "Truly I tell you, I don't know you."

As believers, we are to follow closely after Christ, keeping His words alive in our minds and hearts. We develop our love for Him by placing Him first, above all else, by seeking to know Him and to understand His ways. The intimacy of our relationship with Him is the oil within our lamps. Intimacy with Christ is developed through scripture, prayer and worship.

Intimacy with the Father, Son and Holy Spirit should be the driving force of our Christian life. Our intimacy, this oil that we purchase by spending time with Him, keeps us alert and ready as we wait for His return. In the end, it is our knowledge of Him, our intimacy, that is our salvation.

Consider the intimate nature of some of the names by which God calls Himself. Jesus taught us to pray to God as Our Father. Three times in the New Testament, God is represented as Abba or Papa, indicating the nearness of a daddy. (Mark 14:36, Romans 8:15, Galatians 4:6)

The Lord was Abraham's friend. He remains close to us, closer than a brother (James 2:23, Proverbs 18:24). He is the intimate shepherd in Psalm 23. He the comforter of our sorrows. He is our teacher, the one who whispers in our ear to go this way or to take this path (John 14:26, Isaiah 30:21).

In the book of Hosea, God says that He will be to us as a husband, *Ishi*, so that we will no longer view Him as a taskmaster, or a God of rules. Instead He is the One who keeps covenant and inspires hope (Hosea 2:16). In Deuteronomy 7:9, He is the faithful God, *El Emunah*, keeping His covenant of love to a thousand generations with those who love him and keep his commandments.

He is the Bridegroom in the Song of Solomon and in the Gospels (Matthew 9:15, Mark 2:19 and Luke 5:34). Jesus is the One whose eyes are filled with fire - pure and holy love for His Bride. In Revelation 9, Jesus is the Bridegroom at the culmination of the ages when He sits down for the marriage supper with the saints.

Clearly, the Lord is a relational God who longs to reveal Himself to us. He also longs to know the thoughts of our hearts.

CO-LABORING WITH CHRIST

The second lesson that I learned during months and years of consistent prayer is that when we pray, we co-labor with Christ (who lives in us) in order to pray His will into situations (2 Corinthians 13:5, Galatians 2:20, Colossians 1:27, 1 John 5:14, 1 Corinthians 3:9). This is an important concept because we are not working on our own, rather we are working with Jesus in our prayers for His Kingdom to come and His will to be done.

During the 1990s and early 2000s, I initiated prayer strategies and prayer networks for churches, large and small. From 2005-2018, my husband Sam and I served as the Senior Pastors for Encounter Prayer and Worship Center in Charlotte, N.C. We also hosted a house of prayer from within our church. Looking back, it seems as if I spent these years hidden away in the secret places of God, continuing to learn Biblical patterns of prayer.

A favorite verse during this time is taken from the book of the prophet Isaiah.

> *He wakens me morning by morning; He wakens my ear to listen like one being instructed.*
> Isaiah 50:4

It was from this quiet place of listening that *"The Sovereign Lord (gave Isaiah) a well-instructed tongue, to know the word that sustains the weary"* (Isaiah 50:4). Year after year, I have practiced the skill of seeking the Lord, of searching the things of God by listening, with a desire to have words that will encourage others.

Like King David, my focus was to spend time learning about Jesus. *"One thing I ask from the Lord, this only do I seek: that I may dwell in the house of the Lord all the days of my life, to gaze on the beauty of the Lord and to seek him in his temple"* (Psalm 27:4). Through these years, I continued to learn how to bring God's will about through prayer, praise and declaration.

During these years, I took leadership and participatory roles in city wide prayer gatherings, gatherings like The Response, organized by Doug Stringer; Sacred Assemblies, with my friend Bob Perry; City

Wide Prayer with I Pray America; and prayer gatherings at Billy Graham Center, Charlotte, N.C.

•

Yours is the Voice - Now is the Time!

Stretching back through the millennia, there have been times when the power of God was released into the earth in extraordinary ways that changed the course of history. At these significant junctures, the sounds of clashing cultures heard on earth, reverberated also through the heavens, as God's power came to bear upon the desperate needs of nations. At these points in history, the combination of a sovereign God working through yielded people caused the world to witness shifts from one era to the next.

Men and women, by faith, used their voices to transform culture, shift nations and change the course of history. Here are a few examples from the Bible.

King David used his voice to rally a nation and defeat the enemies of God. His voice, through verse and song, has impacted people throughout the world for over three thousand years.

Elijah used his voice to declare God's power, confronting the wickedness of false teachers in Israel. He preserved righteousness and transformed culture.

Daniel used his voice like an arrow to pierce the darkness of a pagan culture. He proclaimed the sovereignty of The Lord over the seasons of men and the dominance of His Kingdom over all.

Esther, from within the palace walls, used her voice to call a nation to pray. She petitioned a mighty king and saved a nation through her obedience.

Nehemiah lifted his voice in confession of national sins, weeping over them. God strengthened him to rebuild the burned and broken walls of Jerusalem.

John the Baptist described himself as "a voice crying out… prepare the way of the Lord!"

The new decade into which we entered in 2020 coincides with the year 5780 in the Hebrew calendar. This is the decade and the year of the Voice.[1]

It is possible that we now have entered into a new era in the history of man. God will support our desires to seek first His kingdom and His righteousness.

As we seek God, we can gain an understanding of His will which we can give voice to through prayer. When we pray in faith, God will act on our behalf.

It's time to lift our voices!

Chapter 2: The Call

CULTURE AT A CROSSROADS

Culture is defined as the customs, social institutions and achievements of a nation, people, or other social group.[2] This includes government, arts, education, media, religion, family and business.

During the last century, a great clash of ideologies has intensified in our nation as various groups, with contrasting principles, seek to dominate culture. Public debate and political discord have now reached a fever pitch.

> *See, darkness covers the earth and thick darkness is over the peoples.* Isaiah 60:2

In each day's reporting of the news, we see indications of the darkness that covers our nation. Due to the enormity of the issues and the depravity of sin, our tendency is to turn away. We do our best to ignore America's problems, as we hope to live our lives unscathed and unharmed.

Darkness *has come* to America as we have turned from moral absolutes and embraced moral relativism. As we have turned away from the truths of Scripture and resisted the boundaries that the Lord instituted for our good, social ills have escalated.

Families are in shambles. Millions of Americans struggle with anxiety and depression. Suicide rates are at an all-time high (up 33% from 1999-2017.)[3] As a society, we spend 47 billion dollars a year in the war against drugs, as opioid and other addictions claim lives and shatter families.[4] Americans are increasingly faced with senseless violence, leaving our most vulnerable threatened and afraid.

Advancements in technology, things that were intended to make our lives easier, have now entrapped us with addictions. As time passes, we grow more and more suspicious of the integrity of providers.

In terms of our federal government, it has ballooned beyond the bounds of the Constitution. Our federal institutions are fraught with corruption and inefficiency. Our liberties are threatened because we no longer understand their origin or the nature of the government that was instituted to defend them.

•

America now stands at crossroads. It feels like a distinct moment in time where two roads stretch out before us and we face the choice of which road we will take.

One road is the road of humility before God. It is the road where we wake up and see our nation as it is before the Lord. It is a road on which we recognize our deep need for a return to righteousness. It is the road of individual and corporate confession and repentance. It is a road that has, along its way, restoration, rebuilding and hope. It is a road where God smiles upon us and shows us His favor. It is a road where we serve God in truth, not only by mental assent, but from the depths of our very being.

The other road is a less hopeful one. It is the road of continued and continual strife, dissension and disunity. It is the road of crisis:

intense difficulty, trouble or danger. Along this road, we see the disintegration of our government and our culture. It is a road of chaos and fear. It could very well be a road of bloodshed, of famine, even war. In short, its results are disastrous.

We live within an illusion, if we believe that what happens on the national stage does not, or will not in the future, affect our church communities and our individual lives. For too long, we have turned away from many of our larger cultural problems, seeking refuge in comfortable spaces, or feeling helpless to make a difference. America currently faces the real threat of widespread civil unrest.

In this prayer guide, we will be crying out to the Lord for ourselves, our families, our communities and our nation. We will be asking God to intervene, to help us in our time of need.

Through it all, I hear the call of the Father to return. The Lord makes it very simple:

> *Therefore, tell the people: This is what the LORD Almighty says: "Return to me...I will return to you."*
> Zechariah 1:3

MORALITY AND RELIGION

The Bedrock of American Culture

When the English first reached the shores of Virginia in 1607, intent on establishing a permanent colony, they placed a Christian cross on the beaches of the newly named Cape Henry. This cross was placed in gratitude to God and served as a cultural symbol of the value system that they hoped to bring to this new land.

In 1620, when the English Separatists reached the shores of Massachusetts, while still upon the Mayflower, they drafted a document for the rules of governing this new colony. *The Mayflower Compact* began with these words, "In the Name of God," and expressed the purpose of their endeavors "for the Glory of God and the advancement of the Christian faith, in honor of King and Country a voyage to plant a colony." These pilgrims signed a solemn oath and swore to uphold the governing principles of the compact they had written. Governor William Bradford's personal diary describes the deep and abiding faith of these pilgrims who left their native land in pursuit of religious freedom.

At the founding of our republic, regardless of the personal faith of our individual founding fathers, the leaders of our young nation held a Judeo-Christian worldview. They knew that religion and a strong moral code were the safeguards of our republic.

George Washington said, "Of all the dispositions and habits which lead to political prosperity, religion and morality are indispensable supports."[5]

John Adams declared, "Our constitution was made only for a moral and religious people. It is wholly inadequate to the government of any other."[6]

John Jay, First Chief Justice of U.S. Supreme Court, wrote, "The most effectual means of securing our civil and religious liberties is, always to remember with reverence and gratitude the Source from which they flow."[7]

Historian James Hutson writes that, "Jefferson and Madison fought fiercely for beliefs that 'all men are equally entitled to the free exercise of religion, according to the dictates of conscience,' a natural right which had not previously been recognized as such by political bodies in the Christian world."[8]

Dr. Benjamin Rush, during the Pennsylvania Convention in December 1787 suggested, "that the hand of God was surely employed in the drafting the Constitution as it was in dividing the Red Sea or in fulminating the Ten Commandments from Mount Sinai."[9]

The Judeo-Christian worldview was so strong, that Thomas Jefferson, John Hancock and George Washington each called for days of prayer and fasting before the Lord (documented in following pages).

A Hunger for Righteousness

When I survey the current spiritual landscape of America, I see *a strong hunger* within God's people to see righteousness restored. I hear it in the prayers of many with whom I pray, people like Intercessors for America. I see it in prayer initiatives for Washington, D.C: Dutch Sheets, Cindy Jacobs, Lou Engle and many others leading the way. I see it in the young people who participate in houses of prayer in cities across the nation, giving themselves to extended periods of prayer and worship. I see it in the city-wide gatherings held in many cities.

This year, many thousands each week are attending public gatherings in cities across the nation. Led by Franklin Graham, he exhorts Americans to love and serve the Lord and to participate in civil affairs.

In the pioneering state of Tennessee, on October 10, 2019, Governor Bill Lee called for a public day of prayer and fasting. Church leaders in Nashville, TN and the surrounding suburbs are leading the way with city-wide networking for days of prayer.

I also see it in the public square, as people participate in missions for social justice by serving the poor and standing up for the less fortunate. You can hear it in the cries for refugees and see it in brave men and women who work against human trafficking. I hear it in the passionate prayers of millennials who are taking action to bring change to their cities.

Jesus describes this type of hunger in the parable of the persistent widow. His story is instructive for us today:

> *Then Jesus told his disciples a parable to show them that they should **always pray and not give up**. He said: "In a certain town there was a judge who neither feared God nor cared what people thought. And there was a widow in that town who kept coming to him with the plea, 'Grant me justice against my adversary.' For some time, he refused. But finally he said to himself, 'Even though I don't fear God or care what people think, yet because this widow keeps bothering me, **I will see that she gets justice**, so that she won't eventually come and attack me!'" And the Lord said, "Listen to what the unjust judge says. And will not God bring about justice for his chosen ones, who cry out to him*

*day and night? Will he keep putting them off? I tell you,
He will see that they get justice, and quickly."*
Luke 18:1-8

The widow wanted justice from an unrighteous judge, so she persisted in her pleas until the judge answered her.

Jesus knew that His followers would face challenges. He knows that we often face difficult seasons in our lives and trying times within culture. He exhorts His children to follow this pattern: *always pray to Him and do not give up!*

Because God is just, we can have confidence that He will act on our behalf, but we must be tenacious, not growing weary, and never giving up.

A SEASON OF GRACE

God is now extending a Season of Grace to America, a space in which we might return. The prophet Isaiah tells us to "*Seek God while He may be found.*" He tells us to "*call upon Him while He is near*" (Isaiah 55:6).

Even though God is ever present, there are seasons when *He bends low* to hear our prayers. The great Hebraic blessing bids God to turn His face towards us.

The Lord bless you and keep you;
the Lord make his face shine on you and be gracious to you;
the Lord turn his face toward you *and give you peace.* Numbers 6:24-26

In the course of the history of nations, there have been certain junctures where *God has allowed* a season of grace. These particular junctions **preceded or protected societies** from **cataclysmic change**. The United States is currently in one of those seasons, where God's grace is extended to us, with *an invitation* to humble ourselves and return to Him.

It is important to be aware of the fact that seasons have a beginning and an end. I believe there is, right now, an open window in which grace flows from heaven, offering us a season in which to repent. There is a beam of light that is shining upon us, but it is of vital importance that we discern what the Lord is saying and respond to Him.

Jesus is reaching out to us with great compassion.

> *Is not* [America] *my dear son, the child in whom I delight? Though I often speak against him, I still remember him. Therefore, my heart yearns for him; I have great compassion for him, declares the Lord.*
> Jeremiah 31: 20

> *I have loved you with an everlasting love; I have drawn you with unfailing kindness.*
> Jeremiah 31:3

> *They will come with weeping; they will pray as I bring them back. I will lead them beside streams of water on a level path*

where they will not stumble, because I am (Israel's) father.
Jeremiah 31:9

In the book of Revelation, Jesus says, "*Behold I stand at the door and knock. If anyone hears My voice and opens the door, I will come in and dine with him and he with Me*" (3:20 NASB).[10] The Lord is knocking at our hearts with a desire to come into our lives; with a desire to use us to impact culture. The question is: Will we respond?

Gifts of Faith

I believe that God is freely giving powerful, history-altering gifts of faith to His sons and daughters at this time.

Faith is the currency of heaven.

Faith occurs when we take the Lord at His word.

Faith is described as the "confidence we have in the things that we hope for" (Hebrews 11:1). It is *having an assurance* of something in the spiritual realm that we do not yet see with our eyes.

The Lord is drawn to our faith. He turns His face towards us and hears our prayers when we stand in our belief that He is powerful, willing and able to help us.

During this time, The Lord is extending immeasurable faith to those who will open their hearts to receive from Him. He is giving this free gift of faith - to those who are hungry. These gifts of faith will be given to us so that we *can pray bold prayers and take bold action.* Our faith can bring change to the cultural institutions of our nation.

Returning to the parable of the persistent widow, Jesus asks, **"When the Son of Man comes, will he find faith on the earth?"** (Luke 18:8). **This is the question of the hour.**

Will you reach out to God and ask Him for the gift of faith to pray bold prayers?

A Return to Truth

II Kings, chapter 22, relates the story of the *rediscovery* of Scripture that had been lost in a time when the temple in Jerusalem was in disrepair. As King Josiah's men were supervising the repairs of the temple, the High Priest Hilkiah said, "I have found the book of the Law in the temple of the Lord." II Kings 22:8. Hilkiah read this book to the private secretary of the King, who then read God's word in the presence of the King Josiah. When Josiah heard the words of the book, he tore his robes as a sign of humility because his heart burned within him as he heard God's truth.

In large measure, within our current religious culture, there has been a rejection of God's truths in favor of a man-centered gospel. As J. Gresham Machen states, "When doctrine and truth are abandoned, you don't get liberal Christianity, you get another religion altogether."[11]

In many ways, an awakening is the rediscovery of eternal truths. The arrows in this book will point towards truth through the lens of a Biblical worldview.

To summarize:

- **God is stirring a hunger for righteousness** within His people.
- **God is extending to us a season of grace**, a window in time, during which we might consider our ways and make choices that change our direction.
- **Jesus stands at the door and knocks**, with a desire to come into our communities.
- **We must respond with a sense of urgency.** We have a participatory role and a responsibility to facilitate revival through our prayers: we must cry out to Him day and night.
- **God will give the gift of faith** to those who ask; this power will change the course of our communities and our country.
- **Awakening is a rediscovery of eternal truths.**
- **The Lord will act on our behalf when we cry out to Him.**

Dependent Upon Us

In many ways, revival and awakening, transformation and survival of society- as we know it- are dependent upon our response to the principle of II Chronicles 7:14. *If my people, who are called by my name, will humble themselves and pray and seek my face and turn from their wicked ways, then I will hear from heaven, and I will forgive their sin and will heal their land.*

Chapter 3: Days of Prayer and Fasting

America's Tradition of Prayer and Fasting

As early as 1620, we see the roots of proclaimed days for communal fasting. William Bradford records, "I proclaimed a fast that we might humble ourselves before our God, and seek of Him a right way for us and for our children, and for all our substance."[12] Later, in the Massachusetts Bay Colony (Boston), the Puritans proclaimed days of corporate fasting in 1644, 1645, 1647, 1648.[13]

In the 1750's, Americans returned to the zeal and love for God that was so much a part of early colonial life. Instrumental to these revivals were men like Jonathan Edwards, Samuel Davies and Gilbert Tennent. God used an extraordinarily gifted orator, George Whitefield, to preach the Gospel to the colonists who lived up and down the Eastern Coast of America. Hundreds of thousands of men, women and children came to Christ. Church attendance swelled, new churches and new Christian colleges were established during this time. The First Great Awakening brought to Americans a sense of individuality and independence because the message that was preached focused on individual accountability to God alone, without the intervention of church and clergy. Although familiar to us, this was a radical departure from thousands of years of tradition. The First Great Awakening laid a foundation for the quest for liberty that would culminate in revolution.

As early as 1774, in our quest for independence, the leading voices in the colonies called for days of prayer and fasting. On June 1, 1774, in their struggles against the British Crown, Thomas Jefferson drafted a "Day of Fasting," and introduced it to the Virginia House of Burgesses. It was supported by other representatives, by Patrick Henry, Richard Henry Lee and George Mason. The resolution passed unanimously.[14]

George Washington, participating in the fast, wrote in his diary on June, 1774: "Went to church, fasted all day."[15]

On April 15, 1775, John Hancock, called for a day of prayer and fasting, declaring, "In circumstances dark as these, it becomes us, as men and Christians, to reflect that, whilst every prudent measure should be taken to ward off the impending judgments, the 11th of May next be set apart as a Day of Public Humiliation, Fasting and Prayer to confess their sins to implore the Forgiveness of all our Transgression."[16]

After the Continental Congress passed a resolution for a Day of Public Humiliation, Fasting and Prayer, John Adams wrote to his wife, Abigail, on July 12, 1775: "We have appointed a Continental fast. Millions will be upon their knees at once before their great Creator, imploring His forgiveness and blessing; His smiles on American Council and arms."[17]

After the Battles of Breed's Hill, during the siege of Boston, Colonel Knox's cannons from Fort Ticonderoga were placed on Dorchester Heights overlooking the docked British ships. General Washington then ordered, on March 6, 1776, that, "Thursday, the 7th be set apart by this Province as a Day of Fasting, Prayer and

Humiliation, 'to implore the Lord and Giver of all victory to pardon our manifold sins and wickedness, and that it would please Him to bless the Continental army with His divine favor and protection,' that day to the sacred duties due to the Lord of hosts for His mercies already received, and for those blessings which our holiness and uprightness of life can alone encourage us to hope through His mercy to obtain."[18] Unable to defend his position, British General Howe was forced to abandon his plans of attacking the cannons on Dorchester Heights. The British soon evacuated Boston in defeat.

The founding fathers knew, first, that a dependence upon God was necessary for the well-being of our nation. In July, 1776, "For the support of this Declaration, with *a firm reliance on the protection of divine Providence*," the signers "pledged their lives, their fortunes and their sacred honor" and attached their names to the Declaration of Independence.

The following is a proclamation that calls for a public day of prayer and fasting by President John Adams in 1799. It reads like a Psalm of devotion. It is incredibly potent for our present circumstances.

> "I do hereby recommend accordingly, that Thursday, the 25th day of April next, be observed throughout the United States of America as a day of solemn humiliation, fasting, and prayer; that the citizens on that day abstain as far as may be from their secular occupations, devote the time to the sacred duties of religion in public and in private; **that they call to mind our numerous offenses**

against the Most High God, confess them before Him with the sincerest penitence, implore His pardoning mercy, through the Great Mediator and Redeemer, for our past transgressions, and that through the grace of His Holy Spirit we may be disposed and enabled to yield a more suitable obedience to His righteous requisitions in time to come; that He would interpose to arrest the progress of that impiety and licentiousness in principle and practice so offensive to Himself and so ruinous to mankind; that He would make us deeply sensible that "righteousness exalteth a nation, but sin is a reproach to any people;" that He would turn us from our transgressions and turn His displeasure from us; that He would withhold us from unreasonable discontent, from disunion, faction, sedition, and insurrection; that He would preserve our country from the desolating sword; that He would save our cities and towns from a repetition of those awful pestilential visitations under which they have lately suffered so severely, and that the health of our inhabitants generally may be precious in His sight; that He would favor us with fruitful seasons and so bless the labors of the husbandman as that there may be food in abundance for man and beast; that He would prosper our commerce, manufactures, and fisheries, and give success to the people in all their lawful industry and enterprise; that He would smile on our colleges, academies, schools, and seminaries of learning, and make them nurseries of sound science, morals, and religion; that He would bless all magistrates, from the highest to the lowest, give them the true spirit of their station, make them a terror to evil doers and a praise to them that do well; **that He would preside over the councils of the nation at this critical period, enlighten them to a just discernment of the public interest, and save them from mistake, division, and discord**; that He would make succeed our preparations for defense and bless our armaments by land and by sea; **that He would put an end to the effusion of human blood and the accumulation of human misery among the contending nations of the earth by disposing them to justice, to equity, to benevolence, and to peace; and that he would extend the blessings of knowledge, of true liberty, and of pure and undefiled religion throughout the world.**"[19]

Upon the request of the U.S. Senate, Abraham Lincoln declared April 30, 1863 as a day of fasting:

"Whereas, the Senate of the United States, devoutly recognizing the Supreme Authority and just Government of Almighty God, in all the affairs of men and of nations, has, by a resolution, requested the President to designate and set apart a day for National prayer and humiliation. **And whereas it is the duty of nations as well as of men, to own their dependence upon the overruling power of God, to confess their sins and transgressions, in humble sorrow, yet with assured hope that genuine repentance will lead to mercy and pardon; and to recognize the sublime truth, announced in the Holy Scriptures and proven by all history, that those nations only are blessed whose God is the Lord...... It behooves us then, to humble ourselves before the offended Power, to confess our national sins, and to pray for clemency and forgiveness."** The proclamation concludes, "All this being done, in sincerity and truth, let us then rest humbly in the hope authorized by the Divine teachings, that the united cry of the Nation will be heard on high, and answered with blessings, no less than the pardon of our national sins, and the restoration of our now divided and suffering Country, to its former happy condition of unity and peace."[20]

These few samples of primary documents speak directly to the belief of the founders in the intervention of Almighty God in the affairs of men, by means of prayer. Jefferson, Washington, John Adams, Madison, John Jay and Patrick Henry all called for and participated in days of consecration and prayer.

Continuing the traditions of Days of Consecrated Prayer into the modern era, Presidents McKinley, Coolidge and Franklin Delano Roosevelt and others called National Days of Prayer and Fasting, with President Roosevelt leading the nation in prayer during a radio address as the Allied troops landed on the beaches of Normandy. The tradition of a call to prayer by our Presidents continues to this day.

These moments in our nation's history mark times of desperation. Men and women fasted in times of crisis - to hold off famine, to seek God's aid in battle, asking God's intervention during our civil war. It is time to seek God's favor once again.

Traditions Become Alive

At this time, God is calling His People to days of consecration, prayer and fasting.

> Prayer and fasting invites God into our circumstances. As we humble ourselves, we ask God to bring His supernatural power to bear upon forces that oppose His will and His blessing.

JOEL 2 - CONGREGATIONAL PRAYERS

During the years that Sam and I were senior pastors, there were several years that I focused my intercession on passages from the book of Joel. Chapter 2 begins with the prophet describing a great and terrible day where darkness covers the earth, even deep darkness. It was a day when the locusts ate all of the harvest of a people who were dependent upon that harvest for their very survival! In the midst of the destruction, *the Lord calls* His people *to return to Him…*

> *"Even now," declares the Lord, "return to me with all your heart, with fasting and weeping and mourning. Rend your heart and not your garments." Return to the Lord your God, for he is gracious and compassionate, slow to anger and abounding in love, and he relents from sending calamity. Who knows? He may turn and relent and leave behind a blessing.*
>
> Joel 2:12-14

The prophet Joel declares:

> *Blow the trumpet in Zion, declare a holy fast, call a sacred assembly, Gather the people, consecrate the assembly; bring together the elders, gather the children, those nursing at the breast. Let the bridegroom leave his room and the bride her chamber.*
>
> Joel 2:15-16

The piercing sound of the trumpet called the people to gather. It served as a call to every person - young and old, to the strong and to the weak. It called everyone out of their chambers, out of their comfortable places.

The call was a somber one, even a dire one. To choose to answer the call, or to neglect its call, could mean the difference between survival and destruction.

The call of the book of Joel is the very desperate call to believers to pray for a nation in need.

> *Let the priests, who minister before the LORD, weep between the portico and the altar. Let them say, "Spare your people, LORD. Do not make your inheritance an object of scorn, a byword among the nations. Why should they say among the peoples, 'Where is their God?'"*

Joel 2: 17

These very powerful words are cries to the Lord for His very presence to remain with them. They are prayers of intercession so that He would spare His people from the consequences of the rebellion of their hearts.

GOD COMMANDS A HOLY FAST, A SACRED ASSEMBLY!

During the time that I was praying these prayers on a weekly basis, I had some conversations with a long- time friend who lives in Nashville, Tennessee. His name is Bob Perry, founder of Worship City Prayer and Integrative Prayer Solutions. Bob was, at that time, leading daily conference calls with Joel 2 as the central text. I began to co-labor with intercessors from the Nashville area.

The work that is going on in the Prayer Movement in Nashville, TN is powerful and profound. Local pastors are working in coordination with civil government leaders to pray for their city. Worship centers and houses of prayer are being established. It is beautiful to see God's work in Nashville, work that is due to the sacrifices of countless individuals and groups.

During this time, Pastor Steve Berger, the Senior Pastor of Grace Chapel, Franklin, TN, recognizing that the means to the general welfare of our nation lie beyond our own capacity, was spearheading gatherings of citizens for the purpose of prayer and fasting. Pastor Berger called these city-wide gatherings, Sacred Assemblies.

A county-wide day of prayer and fasting was to be held in Manchester, TN, in Coffee County, on March 8, 2015. During the preliminary planning meetings, I made several trips to Coffee County to gather with city leaders. Marilyn Howard, the founder of Alabaster House of Prayer, along with government officials, pastors and lay leaders have initiated a prayer movement in their town. They are making a difference for the residents of Coffee County. Along with prayer, these faithful leaders host an evangelistic outreach each year to the more than 80,000 attendees at the annual Bonnaroo Music Festival. This is a beautiful example of the prayer movement, working in coordination with evangelistic outreaches.

I had the privilege of joining the Coffee County residents for the Sacred Assembly in 2015. The Assembly itself was held on the steps of the Court House in Manchester. City and County leaders, pastors from different congregations, as well as hundreds of citizens gathered together in humility and repentance in prayer to the Lord.

These types of Sacred Assemblies have been held in many formats, in many towns and cities, across the United States. They are times when people come together in prayer, fasting and repentance for our nation. I have participated in The Response, led by Doug Stringer, in both Houston, Texas, in 2011 and in Charlotte, in 2015.

Isaiah 58 – An Acceptable Fast

In general, fasting draws us closer to God. As the strength of our flesh is diminished, we are made more aware of the reality of the spiritual realm.

Isaiah, chapter 58, gives us insight into the significance that the Lord places on prayer and fasting. As you read these verses, consider the instructions, as well as the promises within. Look for the keys to restoration that God provides for us, both for our individual lives and our families, as well as for our communities and our nation. Take time to read, afresh, these verses written by the prophet Isaiah:

> *Is this the kind of fast I have chosen, only a day for people to humble themselves? Is it only for bowing one's head like a reed and for lying in sackcloth and ashes? Is that what you call a fast, a day acceptable to the Lord?*
> Isaiah 58:5

The first aspect to understand about fasting is that this practice places us in a posture of humility and dependence upon the Lord. We willingly put ourselves in the correct posture of humility. We ask God to open our eyes, so that we might begin to understand God's perfection and our need for Him. When we fast, we can begin to understand how vast is the wisdom and might of the Lord and how woefully short we fall in our understanding. In fasting, we declare our complete dependence upon God:

> *Is not this the kind of fasting I have chosen: To loose the bonds of wickedness, To undo the heavy burdens, To let the oppressed go free, And that you break every yoke?*
> Isaiah 58:6

When we fast, we think not only of ourselves and our needs, but also about the needs of others, about those who are in bondage to sin and darkness. We intercede for the freedom of others. We fast so that we can discern the needs of others and extend our hands to meet needs.

> *Is it not to share your food with the hungry and to provide the poor wanderer with shelter—when you see the naked, to clothe them.*
> Isaiah 58:7

As we fast, when we humble ourselves and intercede for others, the Lord promises us restoration.

> *Then your light will break forth like the dawn, and your healing will quickly appear; then your righteousness will go before you, and the glory of the Lord will be your rear guard. Then you will call, and the Lord will answer; you will cry for help, and he will say: Here am I. The Lord will guide you always; he will satisfy your needs in a sun-scorched land and*

will strengthen your frame. You will be like a well-watered garden, like a spring whose waters never fail.
Isaiah 58:8-11

When we pray and fast, we become God's agents of change. We will be reformers, repairers, those who restore our cities.

Your people will rebuild the ancient ruins and will raise up the age-old foundations; you will be called Repairer of Broken Walls, Restorer of Streets with Dwellings.
Isaiah 58: 12

In Isaiah 58, the Lord invites us into the supernatural. As we share in suffering, on the behalf of others, we will see God's power at work: setting others free, restoring us and releasing us as reformers to our cities. These are God's faithful and true promises to us.

Psalm 113:5,6 says, "*Who is like the Lord our God, who is enthroned on high, who humbles Himself to behold the things that are in the heavens and in the earth?*"(NASB). This verse breaks me of my pride and elicits reverence and worship. Who has a God who is as gracious as this? The Creator of the Universe will see, hear and act *when we act*--when we pray and when we seek His face.

With Gratitude

I am so grateful for the pioneering work of men and women like Dutch Sheets, with Appeal to Heaven; Anne Graham Lotz; Franklin Graham; Cindy Jacobs' Reformation Prayer Network; Mike Bickle, leader of International House of Prayer; Richard Simmons, with Men for Nations and Doug Stringer with The Response.

I am so grateful to community leaders like Pastor Steve Berger at Grace Chapel, Franklin, TN and to others who are taking the lead within their communities to call people to prayer.

Allow these examples of prayer movements within cities to encourage you to pray for your community and for our nation.

•

If you are a community leader, a pastor, an administrator of a Christian school or owner of a business, consider calling for a day of consecration, prayer and fasting on behalf of our nation.

Chapter 4: Poised for an Awakening

I believe that America is poised for an Awakening that will bring thorough and dramatic change to our nation; in short, a transformation.

Awakening occurs in specific moments when we are *confronted with truth and our eyes are opened* to these truths.

The first awakening that occurred in my life was when I realized that the historical Jesus, whom I had heard about all of my life, was alive and real. When I accepted the fact that Jesus died for me, I knew that my sins were forgiven. I turned away from living a life of selfishness and sin towards living a life of devotion to God. In Jesus, I found great joy! My understanding was awakened to the Creator of the Universe, and I knew, then, that God had a purpose for my life.

Over the last months, as I have prayed, 'awakening' sometimes looks like this: My husband and I are praying together, I pray something that seems like so much wisdom; I then ask myself, 'why in the world haven't I been praying that for years, or acting on that?' *That* is God awakening me to truth.

Why hadn't I seen those things in the past? I do not know. Possibly, the answer is as simple as, this is God's timing for Awakening.

Awakening can come in greater measure when communities embrace truth. The United States is a nation that is in great need of a sweeping Awakening. We need *a transformation* of our moral code. This next move requires our participation.

Now, faith is; now, is the time for a transformative move of God in the United States.

An Awakening to Love

I believe that the awakening that God is bringing to America is an awakening to Love.

When we encounter Jesus, we encounter love. It is a love that is rooted in truth; it is uncompromising. It is a love that is unconditional and relentless. It is a love that covered sin and conquered death. God's love restores the broken heart and heals the deepest wounds.

Jesus beckons us to draw near to Him, so that we can experience this love and restoration.

As David Benner writes, "God's love is the source and fulfillment of all creation. From the beginning, God's love has been evoking life in all its abundance. It is the passion—the oxygen, the flame, the glue—fueling, firing, connecting the universe in its amazing array."[21] It is an invitation to love that God extended to us when He sent Jesus to redeem us. It is the invitation to love that God is extending today.

When we pray for others, we must pray from a heart of love.

> "There is no great movement of God that has ever occurred that does not begin with the extraordinary prayer of God's people."
> Dr. Ronnie Floyd

I wrote this book because I think that it is vital that *all believers* take a role in praying for our country. I believe that *the only thing* that will stabilize our culture, at this time, is a sweeping move of God's Spirit, an Awakening that crosses political and denominational lines, reaches across socio-economic and ethnic barriers, and brings transformation to our nation.

OBSTACLES TO PRAYER

Consider what might keep you from prayer... First, sometimes people feel that they don't know how to pray. They don't know where to begin their conversations with God. They might feel awkward. This book will help you to begin.

Second, we must have faith that God is listening. He is! The Bible tells us that His ears are open to our cries (Psalm 34:15). It is in His nature and within His character to hear us and to act on our behalf. Keep reading!

Third, we need to create habits. Start small. Make a small goal of praying five or ten minutes a day. You can do that!

Fourth, we need faith-- belief that our prayers make a difference. If we count the cost of not praying, if we look around us and see the tension in our government; the strife and hatred in our dialogue; the depravity in our entertainment culture; our misplaced trust in who we choose as persons of influence, we must throw ourselves upon the mercy of God-- and trust.

Fifth, we must deal with personal weaknesses - our apathy and our desires for other things. It is possible that, because we serve God in various other capacities, we think that we are exempt from the responsibility of stewarding our nation through prayer and service.

Other barriers may be: We simply might not be hungry enough. Complacent in our liberties and ignorant of the volatile nature of government, we might be too filled and too comfortable to take action.

We might not see the state of our nation as clearly as we need to. We might not recognize the spiritual forces that are working against righteousness - at the highest levels.

While we might see these things, we may feel helpless to combat the moral slide. But the truth is we are not without a Helper. We are not without a Warrior.

A Prayer Strategy That Will Help

Praying in Small Groups

In my years of being a Christian, I have sought out prayer partners. My husband and I make it a priority to pray together. In addition, one of the most fruitful, productive formats of prayer for me is to gather with one or two friends on a weekly basis, at a designated time and place, for the purpose of prayer. I have done this for many years. Even when I had four young children, I prioritized this weekly prayer meeting.

I find that having prayer partners is conducive to growing in prayer, as well as supportive of a consistent prayer life. There is multiplied power in our agreement according to God's word, *"Again, truly I tell you that if two of you on earth agree about anything they ask for, it will be done for them by my Father in heaven. For where two or three gather in my name, there am I with them"* (Matthew 18:19-20).

Please consider God's invitation to you to create a Prayer Circle. Consider asking one, two or three people to gather with you to pray for America at this time.

PATTERNS OF SUCCESS: LESSONS FROM THE BOOK OF DANIEL

We have been given patterns of success and His promises to stand on. We can look to the heroes of our faith as examples of those who, in times of crisis, took a stand and shifted the direction of history.

Below are some of the most powerful verses in all of scripture. These are the words of Daniel as he stood before the king.

> *Let the name of God be blessed forever and ever, for wisdom and power belong to Him. It is He who changes the times and the (seasons) epochs; He removes kings and establishes kings; He gives wisdom to wise men and knowledge to men of understanding. It is He who reveals the profound and hidden things; He knows what is in the darkness, And the light dwells with Him. To You, O God of my fathers, I give*

> *thanks and praise, For You have given me wisdom and power.*
> Daniel 2: 19-23 (NASB)

These declarations of Daniel provide a foundation of faith for prayers that transform culture. Let's unpack them:

"Wisdom belongs to the Lord." The solutions to our problems are found in wisdom - in revealed truth. This wisdom *belongs* to the Lord.

"Power belongs to the Lord." The ability to change circumstances, to alter the story, to bring a different outcome *belongs* to the Lord.

"He changes the times and seasons; He removes kings and establishes them." The Lord, our God, is sovereign over the affairs of men. It is He who changes times, seasons and eras, who removes and establishes rulers and authorities.

"He gives wisdom to the wise and knowledge to the discerning. He reveals the profound and hidden things."

"You have given me wisdom and power." Here is the kicker, for us: God gives wisdom and power to those who seek Him.

The Lord will give us the wisdom and the power that we need in order to change our families and our communities if we seek Him, discern correctly, pray with His power and take action in accordance with His instructions.

You and I can be those who change history. The requirements are willingness, availability, humility, great courage, integrity and faith. All of these attributes are given to men in their relationships with the Lord. All of these attributes, in growing measure, are available to you and me.

Stop and meditate on these powerful words from Daniel 2. Let faith - that your life can make a difference - rise in your heart.

Promises to Stand On

In Scripture, we find many promises that can stand as the foundations for a praying people:

> *If My People who are Called by My Name will humble themselves and pray, and seek My face, and turn away from their wicked ways: then I will hear from Heaven, forgive their sins and will heal their land.*
> 2 Chronicles 7:14

> *Strengthen the feeble hands, steady the knees that give way; say to those with fearful hearts, "Be strong, do not fear; your God will come, He will come with vengeance; with divine retribution. He will come to save you."*
> Isaiah 35: 3-4

> *He who did not spare his own Son, but gave him up for us all—how will he not also, along with him, graciously give us all things?* Romans 8:32

Our prayers will provide the power that is needed to bring Awakening and a seismic shift in our culture, so that we might continue to live in liberty and stability. You can be a person who changes the world with your prayers.

THE CHOICE IS OURS!

In the end, the choice is ours! Will we make the choice to hear God's call to prayer and action, or will we fail to respond?

Like the Israelites of old, the choice remains with us…

> *For this commandment which I command you today is not too mysterious for you, nor is it far off… the word is very near you, in your mouth and in your heart, that you may do it…[22]*
>
> Deuteronomy 30: 11, 14 NKJV

The Lord tell us, in these verses, that His commands are not too mysterious for us. In another translation, God tells us that *His commandments are not too difficult, they are not out of our reach.* They are not far off. Rather, His words are near to us- they are within reach- *so that we can do what God has commanded*! God tells us the choice is ours:

> *I have set before you today life and goodness, as well as death and disaster. For I am commanding you today to love the Lord your God, to walk in His ways, and to keep His commandments, statutes, and ordinances, so that you may live and increase, and the Lord your God may bless you in the land that you are entering to possess.*
>
> Deuteronomy 30:15-16

> *I have set before you: life and death, blessing and cursing;* **THEREFORE, CHOOSE LIFE, that both you and your descendants may live;** *that you may love the Lord your God, that you may obey His voice, and that you may cling to Him, for He is your life and the length of your days; and that you may dwell in the land which the Lord swore to your fathers.* Deuteronomy 30:19-20

The Lord plainly tells us that in order for us to prosper, in order for us to remain in the land, we must choose Him.

> *But if your heart turns away and you do not listen, but are drawn away to bow down to other gods and worship them, I declare to you today that* **you will surely perish; you shall not prolong your days in the land.** Deuteronomy 30:17-18

The Lord is waiting on us. "**Therefore, the LORD longs to be gracious to you, and therefore He waits on high to have compassion on you. For the Lord is a God of justice**" (Isaiah 30:18 NASB). For me, this is one of the most beautiful illustrations of the Lord. In all humility, in all glory, in all of His deep mercy for us, He waits.

Will we respond? Will you?

Chapter 5: Lessons in Prayer

THE MANY FACETS OF PRAYER

Prayer may (or may not) be what you have experienced in the past.

The beautiful thing about prayer is that it is communion. It involves two entities - you and God (or a group of people and God). *Prayer is communication with God* - both speaking and listening. The wonderful thing about prayer is that God listens and acts, but even more wonderful to me is that God speaks.

Whether we are new to prayer or have been devoted to prayer for many years, we must understand that:

- God is Spirit.
- When we are born again, the Holy Spirit comes to dwell within us. It is from our spirit man that we pray.
- It is within our spirit man that we understand or 'hear' God's voice.

Jesus said, *My sheep will hear My voice*, so we desire to continually grow in our capacity to discern the language of our Shepherd: through scripture, through the voice of His Spirit within us and through images, visions or dreams.

We live in a spiritual world. Citizens of western civilizations, especially we who are living after the Age of Reason, often have a hard time with the concept of the worlds as spiritual, so we need to return to the Bible to gain understanding.

Prayer involves petition, simple prayers that invite God into a need.

Prayer is thanksgiving, honoring God for all that He is and acknowledging all that He does for us. Being thankful positions us in proper alignment with God, as we recognize that all of our blessings come from Him. Our very breath and life, daily provisions, friends and family are gifts. God wants to open our eyes to a deep understanding of the bounty that has been extended to us by His gracious hand.

Prayer is worship and includes adoration, praise and love that overflows from a grateful heart.

Prayer is making declarations with power. The hour is upon the church in which saints, pure and clean, make declarations in faith - declarations that are filled with power. These will prepare the way of the Lord.

Our enemy: The Father of Lies

Christians must recognize that we have an enemy. He is the father of lies. Deception, playing a shell game, shifting focus, using misinformation is his game. He also specializes in fear.

The object of the enemy's fury is the message of the Gospel itself, along with the messengers who preach salvation through Jesus. In this, the United States is a target because of the rare and precious gift of the freedom to practice religion that is in the very framework of our founding charters.

When you pray, pray in the Name of Jesus. As the Name of the Son, it carries the authority of the Father. It carries all of the power of heaven.

Be mindful that you pray with the authority that Christ gave us. "*All authority in heaven and on earth has been given to me. Therefore, go and make disciples of all nations… And, surely, I am with you always, to the very end of the age*" (Matthew 28: 18-20).

Our battle: Not Against Flesh and Blood

We must also understand that our battle is not against flesh and blood; it is a battle that has its origin in the unseen realm, manifesting itself in the realm of ideas, displayed through people. As Christians, our battle is against these thoughts which seek to exalt themselves against the knowledge of Christ.

Our battle is also against powers of darkness in the heavens, and our weapons of warfare are spiritual weapons, like prayer, certainly not physical violence.

Pray in Faith

Therefore, I tell you, whatever you ask for in prayer, believe that you have received it, and it will be yours. Mark 11:24

PRAYING SCRIPTURE

One of the most effective ways to pray is to actually pray scriptures aloud. When we use scripture accurately, for this purpose, we know that we are praying God's will. Also, scripture has inherent power, as it is God's revealed will.

The following Psalms serve as model prayers for us in our journey. You can refer to these verses as you begin to take up the prayer topics that are covered.

Become reacquainted with these words. Meditate on the power of them. From these highlights, let faith arise in your heart!

Igniting our Prayers: Psalms 17 and 18

Psalm 17 is the heartfelt cry of David as he lifts his voice to the Lord, asking for God's aid against his enemies. It is also a statement of the faith that David has in a God who answers prayer.

> ***I call on you, my God, for you will answer me;*** *turn your ear to me and hear my prayer. Show me the wonders of your great love, you who save by your right hand those who take refuge in you from their foes. Keep me as the apple of your eye.*
> Psalm 17:6-9

> *(My enemies) are like a lion that is hungry for prey, like a fierce lion crouching in cover. Rise up, Lord, confront them and bring them down; with your sword rescue me from the wicked. By your hand save me from such people, Lord.*
> Psalm 17:12-13

Psalm 18, written by David, is a tremendously encouraging account of *the response of the Lord to believing prayers.*

David was a man who had a passionate heart. David longed for God Himself. He was a man who wanted to know God as a son knows his father, as a man knows his friend. David's heart burned for God.

David wrote this psalm to give praise to God for saving him. King Saul and his armies were plotting against David, pursuing him and threatening his life. When David passionately cried out to the Lord, God delivered him from his enemies.

This psalm provides a pattern for us. It includes affirmation of who God is in our lives, as well as petition, declarations and thanksgiving. Psalm 18 serves as an example to guide us, as we cry out to God in faith, believing that He will act on our behalf!

Notice the passion of David's heart. He unashamedly declares his love for the Lord! God holds the preeminent place of his affections.

> *I love you, O LORD, my strength. The LORD is my rock and my fortress and my deliverer, my God, my rock, in whom I take refuge, my shield, and the horn of my salvation, my stronghold.*
>
> Psalm 18: 1-2

Here, David makes declarations about who God is to him! When David calls the Lord his rock, he is speaking from his life story. He is speaking from his experiences with God. The Lord is David's rock, the one thing that is stable in his life. David knows that he can depend on God. He trusts in His faithfulness.

The Lord is David's refuge from the storm. He is the place where he can hide from the tumult. And God is his salvation, his saving grace, his help in time of need.

David expresses his faith in God. David trusts that God Almighty will respond to his personal needs.

From that place of intimacy, David called upon the Lord when he was surrounded by his enemies. David knew where to find support that saved.

> **I called to the Lord, who is worthy of praise, and I have been saved from my enemies.** *The cords of death entangled me; the torrents of destruction overwhelmed me. The cords of the grave coiled around me; the snares of death confronted me.*
> Psalm 18: 3-5

God responds to David's prayers.

> *In my distress I called to the Lord; I cried to my God for help. From his temple he heard my voice; my cry came before him, into his ears.*
> Psalm 18: 6

> *The Lord thundered from heaven;* **the voice of the Most High resounded** *(above the turmoil of the enemy).*
> Psalm 18:13

From the throne of heaven, God heard David's cry. God responded with a thunderous voice. God's voice thundered above the turmoil of the enemy. Even so, the Voice of God can enter into the conflicts that we see all around us through our prayers. His voice thunders and stills the threats of our enemies. His voice prevails!

We, like David, can pray in faith, trusting in the one whose name is above every name, both in this age and in the next.

•

My prayer for you: *"I pray that the eyes of your heart may be enlightened in order that you may know…***His incomparably great power for us who believe. That power is the same as the mighty strength he exerted when he raised Christ from the dead and seated him at his right hand in the heavenly realms, far above all rule and authority, power and dominion, and every name that is invoked, not only in the present age but also in the one to come.** *And God placed all things under his feet."* Ephesians 1:18-22

•

David continues-
> *He reached down from on high and took hold of me; he drew me out of deep waters. He rescued me from my powerful enemy, from my foes, who were too strong for me. They confronted me in the day of my disaster, but the Lord was my support. He brought me out into a spacious place; because He delighted in me.*
> Psalm 18: 16-19

The Lord rescued David and brought him out into a broad place of safety. The Lord worked miracles on behalf of *one man who prayed, one man who lifted his voice.*

The Lord delighted in David's prayers because He delighted in David himself.

Even so, God delights in you.

•

My prayer for you: *"I pray that out of his glorious riches he may strengthen you with power through his Spirit in your inner being, so that Christ may dwell in your hearts through faith. And I pray that you, being rooted and established in love, may have power, together with all the Lord's holy people,* **to grasp how wide and long and high and deep is the love of Christ, and to know this love that surpasses knowledge**—*that you may be filled to the measure of all the fullness of God."* Ephesians 3:16-19

•

Continuing in Psalm 18, we see how the Lord equipped David with supernatural power - that allowed David to overcome his enemies.

> *29: For by you I can run against a troop, and by my God I can leap over a wall…*
> *32: It is God who arms me with strength and keeps my way secure.*
> *34: He trains my hands for battle; my arms can bend a bow of bronze.*

> *36, 37: You provide a broad path for my feet, so that my ankles do not give way. I pursued my enemies and overtook them; I did not turn back till they were destroyed.*
> *39: You armed me with strength for battle; you humbled my adversaries before me.*

Just as the Lord trained David for warfare, The Lord Jesus continues to teach us how to stand on scripture and how to use His word like a sword to defeat our spiritual enemies.

God gave David *supernatural strength* to fight his enemies, and God expands *our abilities* beyond what we can accomplish in the natural. Our prayers have supernatural power – the same power that raised Jesus from the dead - lives in us.

We are called to release His power through our mouths, just as David did. We are called to implore God to fight for our families, our communities and for our nation.

David ends the song, as he began it, with focus on the One. He praised the Lord!

> *The Lord lives! Praise be to my Rock! Exalted be God my Savior! He is the God who avenges me, who subdues nations under me, who saves me from my enemies. You exalted me above my foes; from a violent man you rescued me. Therefore I will praise you, Lord, among the nations; I will sing the praises of your name. He gives his king great victories; he shows unfailing love to his anointed, to David and to his descendants forever.*

Psalm 18:46-50

David knew that his life, battles and prayers were, not only for his place in the world, but also for the generations to come.

Even so, in this momentous hour, we are praying for our children and grandchildren. We are praying for the generations to come.

Remember these Psalms as you pray. Refer to them and utilize them. Let them be like arrows in your hand, mighty warrior!

Chapter 6: Seven Arrows

Arrows in the Hand of a Warrior

What are the things for which you would be willing to lay down your life?

This is a good question to consider - and to revisit - as the answers to this question provide purpose and boundaries for your life.

Your answer probably includes that you would be willing to lay down your life for loved ones and family members.

What other things would you risk your life for? Would you give your life for your country? Certainly, there are those willing today, and those in our history, who gave their lives for country. Would you give your life for your faith? Certainly, multitudes have been martyred for their faith.

The truth is, some things are worth fighting for; these things should take priority in our lives. They are worthy of our full attention and persistent effort.

For me, those are the things that are outlined in the following pages of this book and designated as *arrows*.

The first and second arrow are coupled together. The first arrow is entitled: *self-government*; and reflects the priority of living a life that is pleasing to Christ. The second arrow is about the institution and cultural building block: *family*.

The third arrow includes prayers for government within *the church* community.

The fourth and fifth arrows address structural elements of our culture: *civil governments (local, state and federal)*.

The sixth arrow is prayer for *media*, freedom and truth within our press. The seventh arrow is prayer for a *Great Awakening* in the United States.

An arrow is a weapon of warfare, as are our prayers. For the warrior, the arrow is valuable, a treasured object, one on which considerable time is spent in its creation. The warrior fashions it to be sleek and sharp, with the capacity to hit the mark. The shaft is designed to be thrust through the atmosphere with as little resistance as possible, with its fletching guiding it to its intended target. The arrowhead should be as sharp as a razor.

By faith, we send forth our prayers as arrows, trusting God that they will hit the mark for which they were fashioned, aiming at characteristics like maturity, restoration, integrity, endurance, truth and belief. Our arrowhead is scripture: God's revealed will and prevailing truth. We pray with belief that our prayers are heard in heaven, that they are effective in taking back ground that has been ceded to the enemy.

How to use 7 Arrows

The remainder of this book is a manual. It is meant to be a tool that you use to support your prayer life.

Each *arrow* contains an essay to provoke thought, as well as scripture. Rather than simply reading through the pages, you may want to stop and ponder the ideas and scriptures. You might want to 'sit with' the material for some time and allow God to do a work in your heart and life. The *first work of prayer* is *to bring a change in us*, a change that makes us more like Jesus.

Each arrow has an aim which provides parameters for our prayers. Also included in each arrow is a brief Prayer Lesson. In each chapter there are scriptures, as well as sample prayers.

•

If you have never, or rarely prayed aloud, consider taking a few minutes each day to pray the prayers that you find within this book, or consider asking a friend about meeting on a weekly basis to begin to pray. Praying with others adds so much strength to us and to our prayers.

If you adhere to the premise of this book - the need for prayer for our nation - please ask yourself if you are *actually praying*. Even as a person who has dedicated my life to prayer, I find that often *I am thinking about issues,* but am *not actually stopping to pray.*

•

This book is meant to be used over months and years, so that you might incorporate prayers for culture into your regular prayer life. As you become more familiar with the material, God may have you focus on a particular subject (on a particular arrow) more than others. Arrows 4, 5 and 6 might be clustered together for greater focus.

You might use each of the seven arrows as prayer topics, one topic for each day of the week.

You can pray for as little as ten to fifteen minutes each day, it can change your life as well as make an impact in bringing God's power and love to America.

In the next pages, we will be exploring many topics, all of which should be viewed through the lens of God's love for all people.

Arrow 1: Self-Government

Aiming at Maturity

America's founders would have framed the idea of government in terms of self-control and self-restraint, rather than in the more modern way that we think of government, as the affairs of the state. These two views of the world are *radically* different.

Inherent in the definition of government are the ideas of stewardship, authority and responsibility. We are stewards of the lives that God gives us. As we reach adulthood, we gain authority and must take responsibility for the choices that we make. Understanding these truths empowers us.

We have been given a conscience, a mind, body, will and emotions to steward. Self-government means that we take responsibility for each of these areas. We are masters of our own lives and responsible for the choices we make.

In scripture we see that Jesus tells us to, "Be perfect, therefore, as your heavenly Father is perfect" Matthew 5:48.

This might sound like a difficult statement, but when Jesus told us that we are to be 'perfect,' as He is 'perfect,' the Greek word used here is Teleios. This word means: to be complete in all parts, mature, whole. "Be perfect (mature, whole, complete) even as I am perfect."

It is the same word used in Ephesians 4:13, "receive the instruction of (ministers of the Gospel) *until we all reach unity in the faith and in the knowledge of the Son of God and become mature"* (teleios*).*

The first steps of our journey, of necessity, must be steps towards mastery of our own lives. God is calling His sons and daughters up to a higher level of accountability.

In order for us to pray effectively for others, especially for larger spheres of culture, our own vessel must be filled with truth and light! As I have humbled myself before the Lord, I realize that my approach to cultural issues is often tainted. I desire to be purified, to see things from the perspective of the Bible, then I will be the kind of vessel that is useful to God and to the community.

On our journey towards maturity, we will focus on these areas.

- Purity
- Gratitude
- Forgiveness
- Surrender

Our prayers in this section will deal more with offering our hearts to the Lord, rather than praying for issues. The Lord prioritizes a healthy and whole heart and soul, over all else. We will be asking God for *pure hearts*, for *hearts of gratitude* and for *forgiving, liberated hearts.*

Purity: without any extraneous and unnecessary elements; free from contamination.

The desire for purity comes from within us. It is a desire to be more like Jesus. *"Beloved, now we are children of God…We know that when He appears, we will be like Him, because we will see Him just as He is. And everyone who has this hope fixed on Him purifies himself, just as He is pure"* (1 John 3:2-3 NASB). The desire to live a life of purity is a desire for more of Jesus.

The Psalmist asks, *"Who may ascend the mountain of the Lord? Who may stand in his holy place?"* and he answers with, the following, *"The one who has clean hands and a pure heart."* Psalm 24: 3,4 We must allow God to search our hearts and to bring purification to our souls.

The Psalmist first exhorts us to have 'clean hands.' God invites us to examine ourselves for behavior patterns that do not honor the Lord. Any action we take that is not pleasing to God should be turned from. We can seek God's grace and empowerment, so that we can turn away from sin.

Second, the purview of purity also includes what is *on the inside* of us. Not only our outward behavior, but rather the internal workings of our minds, our souls - our hearts need the cleansing waters of Jesus. When Jesus corrected the religious people of His time, He said that *they do* all of the right things - that their behavioral choices were good, 'you tithe,' 'you pray' etc., but He rebuked them because there was an *inner cleansing* that was lacking.

The outside of the cup looks clean, but the inside of the cup is dirty or empty, void of true righteousness, mercy and love.

The purification process comes with an amazing promise, that, 'The pure in heart shall see God" (Matthew 5:8). As we take steps on the journey of purification, we can *expect to find great joy*. Our lives will be enriched by the purity that God gives us; our relationships will improve. We will experience Life - found in a relationship with the Living God!

LESSONS IN PRAYER

- Listening to the Holy Spirit in order to respond to Him
- Receiving Forgiveness

Jesus told us that one of the roles of the Holy Spirit is to convict us concerning "sin, righteousness and judgment" (John 16:8). On this day, allow the Holy Spirit to bring to your mind any area of sin that might be in your life.

Here is a good prayer to pray from Psalm 139: 23-24:

> *"Search me, God, and know my heart; test me and know my anxious thoughts. See if there is any offensive way in me, and lead me in the way everlasting."*

Talk to God about the thoughts that come to your mind. **Be open with God** *because* He is gracious and willing to forgive.

It is an important exercise to learn how to *receive forgiveness*, as well as other blessings, from God. **Take time to allow God's love and forgiveness to be made manifest in your heart**.

> *If we confess our sins, he is faithful and just and will forgive us our sins and purify us from all unrighteousness.*
> 1 John 1:9

Prayers

Oh Lord, thank you for your son Jesus, through whom we receive life and the forgiveness of sin. Thank you for the work of the cross that is the sole provision for the cleansing of my sin.

Please show me areas of my life that are not in line with your will and your love. Show me any actions that are not pleasing to you. Please give me the grace to turn away and to choose new paths. Empower me to continue to choose Your ways.

Please cleanse my mind and my heart from impurities.

Thank you that you forgive my sin and cleanse me from unrighteousness, according to Your word. "If we confess our sins, he is faithful and just and will forgive us our sins and purify us from all unrighteousness." 1 John 1:9

Thank you for the cleansing work of Your Holy Spirit. Help me to receive the forgiveness that You offer freely. In Jesus' Name, Amen.

> *To God's elect.... who have been chosen according to the foreknowledge of God the Father, through the sanctifying work of the Spirit, to be obedient to Jesus Christ and sprinkled with his blood: grace and peace be yours in abundance.*
> 1 Peter 1: 1-2

Try to be aware of Holy Spirit's work within your life throughout the week. Allow God to continue to do the work of polishing and refining in your life.

Gratitude: *"Give thanks to the Lord for He is good; His love endures forever"* (1 Chronicles 16:34).

I find that gratitude is more than being thankful for things on a list or being thankful for my blessings. My recent prayer has been to ask God to give me a Heart of Gratitude. When we live without a grateful heart, our vision of all aspects of life will be blurry. But when 'my heart' is tenderized to His Spirit, I will easily recognize God's bounty and mercy towards me, and I can respond to Him with grateful words and thanksgivings that spring from my heart.

> *Always give thanks to God for everything, in the Name of the Lord Jesus Christ.*
> Ephesians 5:20

> *Let them give thanks to the Lord for His unfailing love and for His wonderful deeds for mankind; for He satisfies the thirsty and fills the hungry with good things.*
> Psalm 107: 8-9

Beyond that, every day, I think about how blessed I am to live in a nation whose laws support the rights to liberty and justice.

When I put my head on the pillow, I thank God for the tranquility and peace in which I live, our laws, our servicemen and our police, standing guard over our communities and nation.

I am thankful for our country that protects my rights to make choices: to freely choose who I worship, with whom I gather, where I live, where I travel.

We are free to choose educational and vocational paths for ourselves. We are free to purchase goods and to enjoy the fruit of our labor. We have laws that protect our intellectual, as well as our physical property.

America was the forerunner and a beacon to the world in support of the freedom to gather, to speak, to protest and to worship. Today, Americans enjoy unprecedented and unparalleled liberty and prosperity.

All of our praise for these and our many blessings should be abundant within our hearts and should rise up as grateful prayers and songs to God.

Being grateful:

- Gives praise to the One to whom praise is due
- Puts us in correct alignment with God by recognizing that all gifts come from above
- Reaffirms our dependence upon God
- Releases burdens
- Produces hope
- Increases joy
- Pleases and honors God

Prayers

Father, forgive me for neglecting to give You thanks for all of Your many blessings. Thank you for the beauty and abundance of the earth.

Thank You for daily provision - for daily food and housing. Thank you for all of the material blessings that I enjoy.

(Give thanks for all that the Father brings to your thoughts.)

More than all, Lord, please grant me that I would have a GRATEFUL HEART. Bring me into maturity by creating within me an awareness of all of Your bounty in my life. Grant me a grateful heart. In Jesus Name, Amen.

Forgiveness: to set free; to let go; to release.

Reverend Martin Luther King, Jr. said, "First, we must develop and maintain the capacity to forgive. He who is devoid of the power to forgive is devoid of the power to love." Forgiveness is the path to freedom and to healing in our lives.

During the course of our lives, we have the need of both receiving and of giving forgiveness. Our kind and compassionate Father in heaven extended free and full forgiveness to us by sending His Son Jesus to us. Our beloved Jesus lived a life of complete obedience to the Father, never erring into pride or selfishness or sin. He then suffered greatly in order for us to enjoy unhindered fellowship with the Father. God sent His Holy Spirit into our lives, to live with us, to comfort us and to lead us into truth.

First, take time to **receive the forgiveness of the Lord** in areas of weakness and sin in your life.

Jesus also commanded us to **forgive others** for things that have been done to us and for things that have been left undone.

> "The word '**forgive**' is the Greek word **aphiemi**. It means to set free; to let go; to release; to discharge; or to liberate completely. It was used in a secular sense in New Testament times in reference to canceling a debt or releasing someone from the obligation of a contract, a commitment, or promise. Thus, it means to forfeit any right to hold a person captive to a previous commitment or wrong he has committed. In essence, the word 'forgive'—the Greek word **aphiemi**—is the picture of totally freeing and releasing someone."[23]

When we are hurt by others, or mistreated, our initial response is often anger. We might even be tempted to retaliate. But the Kingdom of God is an upside-down kingdom - the path to healing of our own souls is through forgiveness.

> *Forgive us our sins, as we forgive those who have sinned against us.*
> Jesus of Nazareth

Prayers

Father, please grant me a heart that forgives myself and others. According to Matthew 5:48, make me whole, as You are whole.

You said, forgive us our sins, as we forgive others. Father, I choose to forgive those who have hurt me or injured me in any way. Please bring to my remembrance any offenses that I hold towards individuals, towards my family, or towards any larger community.

(Take time to allow the Holy Spirit to search your heart. Take time for repentance and to release others, forgiving fully.)

Father, heal me of any wounds that I have received from family members. Heal me of wounds that I have received by friends or enemies. I ask You to heal me of any wounding that I have received. Cleanse me and wash me. Remove from me a spirit of offense. Cleanse me of any bitterness. Thank you for releasing me from unforgiveness.

I offer free and full forgiveness to any who have injured me.
In Jesus Name, I pray. Amen.

You, Lord, are forgiving and good, abounding in love to all who call to you. Hear my prayer, Lord; listen to my cry for mercy.
Psalm 86: 5-6

Thank God for the precious blood of Jesus by which we are redeemed.

A Cultural Divide

The act of forgiving applies not only to our personal lives, to our interpersonal relationships, but also to culture at large.

All Americans are susceptible to the cultural bumps and bruises of living within a social group or culture. The Bible commands us to, *"Make sure that nobody pays back wrong for wrong, but always strive to do what is good for each other"* (1 Thessalonians 5:15).

Some of the most obvious and more serious breaches of justice in American history have occurred along ethnic or racial lines. In the study of our history, there was obviously a great clash of cultures between European ethnic groups and Native Americans after Christopher Columbus landed on the Caribbean Islands. The natives of North America included many different tribes with a variety of distinct cultures. Interaction with natives varied between the Spanish, French and English. In the end, disease decimated the native populations. Europeans conquered those who were living in the Americas incurring lasting pain for Native Americans.

When I taught U.S. history courses, I covered the thread of history of Africans from the beginnings of the Middle Passage in the 1500's through the Civil Rights Movement of the 1950's and 1960's. It was one of the only historical threads for which I made my personal thoughts known to students. It is a topic that I have researched, studied, prayed over and tried to understand. Even though other ethnic groups have encountered prejudice, including Irish, Italians, Chinese and Japanese, the history of African

Americans has been decidedly different from the story of other ethnic groups.

The inability of the founders to come to the conclusion to eliminate slavery from the beginning is what Condoleezza Rice calls America's "birth defect," and indeed it was. It is humanly impossible for men to make amends for the torture that individuals and families endured under the yoke of slavery in America. In truth, it is only the blood of Jesus that is sufficient to heal such deep and devastating wounds. As we know, slavery was made illegal and equal rights were articulated in the 13th, 14th and 15th amendments, but African Americans did not begin to enjoy full and equal rights until the Modern Civil Rights Movement. As Reverend King said in his *I Have A Dream* speech in 1963, one hundred years later, the life of the African American is "still sadly crippled by the manacles of segregation and the chains of discrimination."[24]

Nevertheless, Martin Luther King Jr. believed in the ideals of the Declaration of Independence. He affirmed the belief that our rights are given to us *by our Creator* - the rights to life, liberty and the pursuit of happiness. And he sought reform.
Consider these words from Reverend King, *I Have a Dream*.

> "In a sense we have come to our nation's capital to cash a check. When the architects of our republic wrote the magnificent words of the Constitution and the Declaration of Independence, they were signing a promissory note to which every American was to fall heir. This note was a promise that all men, yes, black men as well as white men, would be

guaranteed the unalienable rights of life, liberty, and the pursuit of happiness."

Rev. King went on to say that this promissory note was returned with insufficient funds towards African Americans, but that with the March on Washington, Americans gathered in the nation's capital "to cash the check and to demand the riches of freedom and security of justice" for African Americans. We must all continue to stand for a society that ensures equal rights for all.

King continued, "In the process of gaining our rightful place, we must not be guilty of wrongful deeds. Let us not seek to satisfy our thirst for freedom by drinking from the cup of bitterness and hatred. We must forever conduct our struggle on the high plain of dignity and discipline."

"I have a dream that one day every valley shall be exalted, every hill and mountain shall be made low, the rough places will be made plain, and the crooked places will be made straight, and the glory of the Lord shall be revealed, and all flesh shall see it together." Through our prayers and acts of reconciliation, we can cause the mountains to be made low and the valleys to be lifted up.

Though your sins are like scarlet, they shall be as white as snow. Isaiah 1:18

Martin Luther King Jr. must have been a man with a lion's heart. In his 1963 sermon, *Love Your Enemies*, King preached, "First, we must develop and maintain the capacity to forgive. He who is devoid of the power to forgive is devoid of the power to love…It is impossible even to begin the act of loving one's enemies without the prior acceptance of the necessity, over and over again, of forgiving those who inflict evil and injury upon us."[25] It takes great courage and strength of heart to forgive where injuries and injustices are great. This courage might only be found within the love of God.

God's eternal truths remain: the remedy for the pain of the human heart is the exchange of love for hate, of forgiveness for sin. Our comfort is that Jesus Himself bore our sins in His body on the cross, and by His stripes, we are healed.

Booker T. Washington wrote beautifully about forgiveness as 'he worked to cease to cherish a spirit of bitterness' and wrote that "Great men cultivate love…only little men cherish a spirit of hatred."

The blood of Jesus can be applied along the fissures and tears of society at large. We can stand in the gap for the sins of our communities.

We pray, as Nehemiah did, in confession of our national sins.
Let your ear be attentive and your eyes open to hear the prayer your servant is praying before you day and night for your servants, the people of (America). I confess the sins we (Americans), including myself and my father's family, have committed against you. Nehemiah 1:6

Prayers

Father, we ask You to forgive our national sins. We thank you that the shed blood of Your son is sufficient to heal hearts and souls. We ask you for healing and restoration of all people. Thank you for answering our prayers for healing and forgiveness.

We pray that love for all people would abound in our nation. Pour out Your love and compassion. Heal our land, we pray.

Assist us with Your wisdom in continuing to make laws that ensure protection of liberties for all. Thank you, In Jesus Name, Amen.

(Allow the Holy Spirit to lead you in prayers for healing of cultural wounds).

Surrender: Jesus says, "Come to Me all who are weary… I will give you rest" (Matthew 11:28).

It is God's desire that we move towards Him in ever-increasing intimacy. When we run towards Him, He meets us with the embrace of a loving Father.

> "Can we give up all for the love of God? When the surrender of ourselves seems too much to ask, it is first of all because our thoughts about God Himself are paltry. We have not really seen Him, we have hardly tested Him at all and learned how good He is. In our blindness we approach Him with suspicious reserve. We ask how much of our fun He intends to spoil, how much He will demand from us, how high is the price we must pay before He is placated. If we had the least notion of His loving-kindness and tender mercy, His fatherly care for His poor children, His generosity, His beautiful

plans for us; if we knew how patiently He waits for our turning to Him, how gently He means to lead us to green pastures and still waters, how carefully He is preparing a place for us, how ceaselessly He is ordering and ordaining and engineering His Master Plan for our good-if we had any inkling of all this, could we be reluctant to let go of our smashed dandelions or whatever we clutch so fiercely in our sweaty little hands? If with courage and joy we pour ourselves out for Him and for others for His sake, it is not possible to lose, in any final sense, anything worth keeping. We will lose ourselves and our selfishness. We will gain everything worth having."[26]

Elisabeth Elliott

When we surrender, we are surrendering to God's grace and love. We can echo the words of Christ when He said, "Not my will, but Yours be done." Luke 22:42

Arrow 2: Family Government

AIMING AT RESTORATION

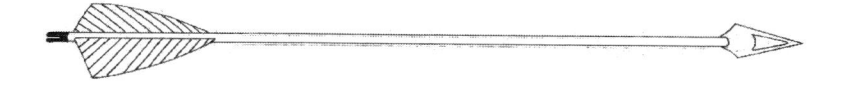

> **Stand at the Crossroads and look; ask for the ancient paths, where the good way is and walk in it, and you will find rest for your souls.**
> **Jeremiah 16:6**

In this section, my goal is to illuminate the forces that are currently assaulting the cultural building block: family, the second sphere of government. While these issues (forces) will be briefly introduced, much more could be written about each of the subjects. *We will be praying for the restoration of the family*, this essential element of our society.

Family is defined as: a collective body of persons who form one household under one head and one domestic government, including parents and children. "The family... is a form of government - established for the good of children themselves - the first government that each of us must obey."[27] Pastor Ryan Carson from Mission Community Church, Charlotte, says that the purpose of family (and church) government is "to protect and to empower."

Throughout history, the family has been the building block of strong societies. This was true of the Hebrew people, the early

Roman Republic, Asian cultures, Anglo-Saxons, the United States and many others. When this building block is strong, strong communities follow. When it is weakened or corrupted, a fragility permeates the larger community and exposes the community, or nation, to destructive forces.

Until the 20th century, Americans accepted, and the body of our laws reflected and supported, the Judeo-Christian view of morality, marriage and family. Since the 1960s, Americans have increasingly accepted a *secular view of the world*. "Secularism is defined as attitudes, activities, or other things that have no religious or spiritual basis."[28]

Currently, America is embracing a secular moral revolution.

As we discuss family, we will be exploring moral issues. It is important to understand that 'every moral system rests on a worldview. Morals are not simply a list of rules.'[29]

For many, the moral issues that will be discussed here are sensitive topics. We all have loved ones who embrace the shifts in family values that we see in our cultural landscape.

My prayer is that we will see the solutions to the assault on the family in the word; "Return:" a return to the first principles, a return to Biblical precepts, a return to the Father.

Scripture tells us that God desires that we know truth in our innermost part (Psalm 51:6). If we are believers in Christ, then we embrace a Scriptural view of all things. We accept God's word as truth.

The sum of God's word is truth, that endures forever.
Psalm 119:160 NASB

For the word of the Lord is right and true.
Psalm 33:4

> **Even though culture changes, God's principles are established and will endure forever.**

God's truths are not meant to be harmful. They are not hateful; neither are those who stand up for truth 'hateful' or bigoted. All of God's work is done in love. (God is love.) All of his boundaries are created *to keep* men, women and children *from harm and pain.*

God's plan for peace in our lives comes through making right choices. It comes through righteous living. You can see this truth exemplified in simple ways in your own life. When your relationships with loved ones are right, you have peace and joy. When you are doing well at work (doing right), you have peace and joy. When you obey the law, you have peace and are undisturbed. When we are living in righteousness, making right choices, we will be at peace with ourselves. One of the scriptures that articulates this concept: "the kingdom of God is righteousness, (then) peace and joy" (Romans

14:17). Conversely, when we stray from God's standards, we will experience anxiety, stress and pain.

As we discuss the following topics, you may find yourself, your story, within the larger story of cultural issues. I assure you that our compassionate Father desires to heal you, comfort you and show you His great love.

Second, we all have loved ones, family members, who are living in some aspects apart from God. My prayer for all of us is that we will continue to walk in truth and speak truth, while showing God's great love. We can love others deeply, and at the same time, not compromise on God's word. Jesus is our example.

As we discuss these issues, remember that it is *always the heart of the Father* to restore. The Lord reaches out to all of us *with great compassion*. He sent Jesus to die for us, even in our sin.

From the book of Jeremiah:

> *Nevertheless, I will bring health and healing to it; I will heal my people and will let them enjoy abundant peace and security. I will bring Judah and Israel back from captivity and will rebuild them as they were before. I will cleanse them from all the sin they have committed against me and will forgive all their sins of rebellion against me. Then this city will bring me renown, joy, praise and honor before all nations on earth that hear of all the good things I do for it; and they will be in awe and will tremble at the abundant prosperity and peace I provide for it.*

Jeremiah 33:6-9

From the book of Joel:
> *Then I will make up to you for the years that the swarming locust has eaten, the creeping locust, the stripping locust and the gnawing locust.*
>
> Joel 2:23-25 NASB

Last, and possibly most importantly, the Lord desires to place within believers the recognition that all people have sinned; hat in this, we are all the same, all in need of the Savior Jesus. May God do the supernatural work of causing us to emanate the fragrance of Jesus, a healing balm to every one is who broken.

The Foundations

God created the world.

As Christians, we recognize that God created the world, the universe and all that is in it. A teleological argument reveals that the "structure, function or interconnectedness"[30] that people see in nature point to the existence of God. All of nature, including man, has purpose. Throughout the millennia, most civilizations held that "reality consists of both a natural and a moral order that are integrated into an overall unity."[31]

When God created man, He said, 'Let us make mankind in our image, in our likeness.'

> *God created mankind in His own image, in the image of God he created them; male and female he created them.*
>
> Genesis 1:26-27

> *God blessed them and said to them, "Be fruitful and increase in number; fill the earth and subdue it. Rule over (the earth)."*
>
> Genesis 1:28

God created man with a purpose.

God created males and females. He blessed them and He commanded them to be fruitful (to have children) and to rule over the earth.

The Lord created families. His intention was that males and females would live together in complementary roles. In their partnership, they would parent children. His intention was that men, women and children would know Him.

When sin entered the world, after this fall, God intended that parents would raise their children in godliness. Fathers and mothers were to provide protective barriers for children, shielding them from evil. Parents were to teach their children about God and raise them in reverence and love for God. David Benner states that, "deep down, something within us seems to remember the garden within which we once existed."[32] He said this in reference to love, but the thumbprint of the heavenly Father remains within us in the form of conscience. From deep within, the truths of God call out to us with desires for fulfillment and our conscience speaks to us about right and wrong.

Forces that Assault the Family Unit

Divorce

From the point of view of Scripture, divorce is the breaking of a covenant that a man and a woman make when they take vows that indicate a life-long, exclusive commitment to marriage. Because God is a covenant-keeping God, the marriage vows represent an extension of Him and reflection of who He is. Keeping Covenant is in God's nature, and God places a high value on our adherence to His patterns.

During the 1970s and afterwards, Americans saw an increase in divorce rates, reaching their highest levels in the 1980s and 1990s. The divorce rate has gone down only because many now choose not to marry. Almost 50% of all marriages in the United States will end in divorce or separation. Researchers estimate that 41% of all first marriages end in divorce. 60% of second marriages end in divorce. The United States has the 6th highest divorce rate in the world.[33]

The psychological effects of a broken home are hard to document. In my role as counselor, I have heard the life stories of hundreds of individuals. Wherever divorce has occurred, it is a prominent factor in emotional stress. Divorce can leave life-long scars.

Issues of Life and Sexuality

Nancy Pearcey, author of eight books on Christian worldview, writes that "Life and Sexuality have become the watershed moral issues of our age." In her enlightening and informative book, *Love*

Thy Body, Answering Hard Questions about Life and Sexuality, Pearcey breaks down the philosophical arguments of our day.

The Christian worldview presents *a wholistic view of a person*, where human life consists of body, soul and spirit. These all work together in unity, creating an individual's authentic self. "Secularists blow apart the connection between scientific and moral knowledge."[34]

The secularist accepts a dualistic view, accepting a split: the body/person split. "This dualism has created a fractured, fragmented view of the human being, in which the body is treated as separate from the authentic self."[35]

As Americans are increasingly accepting a secular moral worldview with a dualistic approach, or a divided approach to the essence of man, this opens the door to arguments in favor of abortion, homosexuality and transgenderism.

Below are some of the results of our shift away from a Christian world view.

Abortion

Most scientists now accept that life begins at conception. Even though the founding ideals of our nation include the right to life, our laws concerning abortion do not protect this fundamental right for the unborn. This is justified by the acceptance of an increasingly secular outlook and dualism where the body is separate from the 'person.' Abortion is justified because of the human/personhood divide. The baby is human, but is considered to be so limited in 'personhood' that he/ she does not qualify as someone who has the right to life, or as someone who has rights that are equal to the mother's.[36]

In 1973, The U.S. Supreme Court decriminalized abortion and since that time, nearly 57 million American babies have been terminated as they grew within the wombs of their mothers. Many of these young mothers naively enter abortion clinics without realizing the devastating emotional consequences that they will experience as the result of their choices. Many young men have felt helpless in the wake of these choices. 57 million babies have died.

Cohabitation

Cohabitation in the United States has increased by more than 1,500 percent in the past half century. In 1960, about 450,000 unmarried couples lived together. Now the number is more than 7.5 million.

According to Barna research, two-thirds of adults believe it is a good idea to live with someone before marriage. 'Millennials', compared to 'Elders', are twice as likely to believe cohabitation is a good idea (72%, compared to 36%).[37]

Contrary to popular belief, "couples who cohabit before marriage (and especially before an engagement or an otherwise clear commitment) tend to be less satisfied with their marriages than couples who do not. These negative outcomes are called the 'cohabitation effect.'"[38]- Meg Jay, *The New York Times*.

Biblical Perspective on Sexuality

Consider these words from I Thessalonians.

> *For you know what commandments we gave you by the authority of the Lord Jesus. For this is the will of God, your*

> *sanctification; that is, that you abstain from sexual immorality; that each of you know how to possess his own vessel in sanctification and honor, not in lustful passion, like the Gentiles who do not know God; and that no man transgress and defraud his brother in the matter because the Lord is the avenger in all these things, just as we also told you before and solemnly warned you. For God has not called us for the purpose of impurity, but in sanctification. So, he who rejects this is not rejecting man but the God who gives His Holy Spirit to you.* 1 Thessalonians 4: 2-7 NASB

"No matter what the current secular philosophy tells them, people cannot disassociate their emotions from what they do with their bodies. In the Biblical worldview, sexuality is integrated into the total person. The most complete and intimate physical union is meant to express the most complete and intimate person union of marriage. Biblical morality is teleological: The purpose of sex is to express the one-flesh covenant in the bond of marriage," Nancy Pearcey.

The book of Romans tells us that *"since what may be known about God is plain to them, because God has made it plain to them. For since the creation of the world God's invisible qualities—his eternal power and divine nature—have been clearly seen, being understood from what has been made."* Romans 1:19-20. The universe shouts that there is a God and that each aspect of nature is created with purpose.

Homosexuality

For although they knew God, they neither glorified him as God nor gave thanks to him, but their thinking became futile.... Even their women exchanged natural sexual relations for unnatural ones. In the same way the men also abandoned natural relations with women and were inflamed with lust for one another. Men committed shameful acts with other men, and received in themselves the due penalty for their error. Romans 1:21-27

"Every practice comes with a worldview attached to it.... Same-sex behavior has a logic of its own.... The person who adopts a same-sex identity must disassociate their sexual feelings from their biological identity as male or female, implicitly accepting a two-story dualism that demeans the human body."[39] Similarly, a transgender person, embracing this dualism and rejecting the whole person approach of Scripture, claims that his biology does not match his personhood.

"By contrast, Biblical morality expresses a high view of dignity and significance of the body."[40]

The Equality Act was passed in the U.S. House of Representatives on May 17, 2019. If approved in the Senate, this legislation would amend Civil Rights laws to explicitly include sexual orientation and gender identity as protected classes. What began as a quest for recognition of civil rights for homosexuals has progressed to the point where other Americans are losing their rights to free speech and to the free practice of religion. Attorney General William Barr said that, "Today, religion is being driven out of the marketplace of ideas, and there is an organized, militant secular effort to drive religion out of our lives."[41]

Consider, for example, the life story of Jon Caldara, who was recently fired from his job as an editorialist at the *Denver Post* for refusing to yield to pressure to write that there are more than two genders. Caldara is a libertarian who is actually in favor of the LBGT cause. "He argued (however) that the AP Stylebook — the Associated Press guide used by many media outlets to determine which words and phrases are appropriate or to be avoided — promotes a progressive bias."

"The AP has updated its style to say that gender is no longer binary and thus declared a winner in this divisive debate," he wrote. "They ruled that, 'Not all people fall under one of two categories for sex and gender.' It's admirable that reporters want to be compassionate to transgender individuals and those transitioning, as we all should be. But AP reporters first have a duty to the truth, or so they say. There are only two sexes, identified by an XX or XY chromosome. That is the very definition of binary. The AP ruling it isn't so doesn't change science. It's a premeditative attempt to change culture and policy. It's activism."[42] This is just one of hundreds of cases where the rights to free speech and the freedom of religion, guaranteed by the First Amendment, are being infringed.

Issues of sexuality are being driven by our entertainment industry and supported by our public education system and by media. For a look at how bad things might be consider these proposed guidelines from the Department of Education for California. These textbooks included "telling kindergartners they could be two genders at once or no gender at all; showing third graders large and close up illustrated pictures of the sex act; introducing fourth graders to sexual fantasies, masturbation, and slang words for sexual organs; and presenting high schoolers with a detailed how-to sex manual that included instructions on anal sex for all sexual orientations, BDSM (bondage, domination, sadomasochism), body fluid (urinating on each other) or blood play." [43] Increasingly, in state after state, public schools are embracing curricula, similar to what is described above, even over the objections of parents.

In 2009, the Department of Education embraced initiatives to promote homosexuality in public schools. Currently, our public schools are encouraged to recognize Bisexual Awareness Day, Sept. 23; LGBQT History month in October; Coming Out Day, Oct. 11 and more. These initiatives are a celebration of secularism.

As Life and Sexuality have become the watershed moral issues of our age, the church must be ready to meet the challenge of leading by being a beacon of truth that emanates from a heart of love.

> On a personal level, "Christians must find ways to communicate to those who struggle with sin of any kind so that they will find refuge in the church. People must be able to trust that churches will protect and nurture the bruised and broken parts of their lives." Nancy Pearcey

Education

Gary DeMar astutely observed that "If we neglect our own personal, family, church and local governing duties, each generation will become more and more dependent upon the 'benevolent' state for care and security."[44]

Education is a part of the stewardship of family.

> *Fathers, do not exasperate your children; instead, bring them up in the training and instruction of the Lord.*
> Ephesians 6:4

> *All Scripture is God-breathed and is useful for teaching, rebuking, correcting and training in righteousness.*
> 2 Timothy 3:16

This is not to say that all families must educate their children in the home, but that it is the responsibility of parents to be aware of their children's education and to make the best possible choices. The current adoption of secular morality has been aided by the national administration of our public-school system. While there are millions of dedicated, hard-working, moral administrators and teachers, whom I honor, our federal government is increasingly adopting a social agenda, that includes the particular narrative of the New Left which found its way into the classroom beginning in the 1960s.

"The philosophy of the schoolroom in one generation will be the philosophy of government in the next," said Abraham Lincoln.

Volumes could be written about the influence of our public education system upon the worldview of our young people. We can trace the trends of particular agendas. On the topic of government, for example, in a recent poll of millennials, half of them responded that they would rather live in a socialist or communist country. This thinking represents a huge shift. There is a direct correlation between adopted curricula within schools and worldview.

Our current educational system needs an overhaul and *a return to first principles of education*. It is important that we pray for our local school systems and remain an active voice in this sphere of influence. Curricula should be examined for biases. Parents should be vigilant to investigate our educational systems for the inculcation of social doctrines that oppose a Christian worldview. Lift your voice!

IMPACTS OF FATHERLESSNESS

Poverty

The single highest contributing factor to poverty is the absence of marriage within a household. Consider data compiled and published in the article, "The Extent of Fatherlessness."

"Children in father-absent homes are almost four times more likely to be at or below the poverty line. In 2011, 12% of children in married-couple families were living in poverty, compared to 44% of children in mother-only families.

In a study of 1,977 children age 3 and older living with a residential father or father figure found that children living with married biological parents had significantly fewer externalizing and internalizing behavioral problems than children living with at least one non-biological parent.

Children who grow up in homes without fathers are:

- More likely to be aggressive
- More likely to be depressed, have low self-esteem and do poorly in school
- More likely to be incarcerated and/or to commit suicide. In addition, one of the most unnerving statistics is that nearly 65% of youth suicides a Fatherless home
- "Fatherless children are at a dramatically greater risk of drug and alcohol abuse."[45]

Assault on Boys

"Almost all of the most recent deadly mass shooters have one thing in common: fatherlessness," says Suzanne Venker. "Deeper even than the gun problem is this: boys are broken," says Michael Ian Black. Increasingly, in our society, it is socially acceptable to demean males.

Pornography Addictions

Perhaps one of the most destructive things to families is rampant addictions to pornography**.** Consider some of the statistics**:**

- "In 2006, estimated revenues for porn industry in the United were just under $13 billion.
- 28,258 users are watching porn every second.
- $3,075. is spent on porn on the internet, every second.
- 88% of scenes in porn films contain acts of physical aggression.
- One in five mobile searches are for pornography.

- 90% of teens and 96% of young adults are either encouraging, accepting or neutral when they talk about porn with their friends.
- 64% of Christian men and 15% of Christian women say that they watch porn at least once a month.
- 51% of male students and 32% of female students first viewed porn before their teenage years." [46]

These statistics are from an organization called Covenant Eyes (CovenantEyes.com) that seeks to support freedom from pornography.

•

In the book of Jeremiah, God asks, why?

> *"Why has this people slidden back, Jerusalem, in a perpetual backsliding?"* Jeremiah 22:5 NKJV

> *And the Lord goes on to say,*
> *"They hold fast to deceit; they refuse to return. I listened and heard; but they do not speak aright.* **No man repented of his wickedness, saying, 'What have I done?' Everyone turned to his own course.***"*
> Jeremiah 22:6 NKJV

The first step toward healing is the recognition that the 'walls' of this basic building block have been burned and are in disrepair. We must not hold on to deceit, but rather recognize our need for God and return to Him with humility.

Often our way forward is to return to ancient paths of truth. *We must be willing to ask God* to show us *His truth and His ways*. With an open heart, we seek Him, asking for His grace.

> **Stand at the Crossroads and look; ask for the ancient paths, where the good way is and walk in it, and you will find rest for your souls.**
> Jeremiah 6:16

SOLUTIONS TO OUR BROKENNESS

From a sociological point of view, "Marriage remains America's strongest anti-poverty, anti-crime, pro-health institution. It is an undeniable fact that the best chances for financial success, emotional well-being, and good health for both parents and children happen when parents are married and families are intact," (Genevieve Wood).

God explains marriage and family through His word, beginning in Genesis when He created people as male and female, and called this good.

Jesus reinforces the idea of marriage, "For this reason a man shall leave his father and mother and be united to his wife, and the two shall become one flesh," (Matthew 19:5).

Again, in scripture, "Marriage is to be held in honor among all, and the marriage bed is to be undefiled; for fornicators and adulterers God will judge," (Hebrews 13:4 NASB).

Behold, I will send you Elijah the prophet before the coming of the great and dreadful Day of the LORD. And he will turn the hearts of the fathers to their children, and the hearts of the children to their fathers. Otherwise, I will come and strike the land with a curse. Malachi 4:5-6

A Move of Power

As we step up to the call to pray for our nation, God will release powerful and lasting change in the hearts of men and women to turn us back to hearth and home.

I continue to hear in my spirit that God wants to do an incredible *work of restoration in the lives of men in our country*. Contrary to what we hear in today's culture, we need to support men with exhortation and encouragement to function in strength and dignity in the way that the Lord created them. We must combat the spiritual assaults against them. Strong, godly men actually provide leadership, security and a covering for their families, just as God intended. As men are restored, they will accurately reflect the image of God.

Along with this, God desires to restore fatherhood. Restoration of the fathers comes as men are connected to the unconditional love of their Father in heaven. When men begin to see themselves as God sees them, then restoration will come. The prophet Malachi declares that God will send 'the spirit of Elijah' to return the hearts of the fathers to the children. Fathers are given a stewardship over their families, and the Lord wants to teach and tutor men on how to lead with great love, commitment and devotion. Godly fathers will protect and empower their wives and children, providing a safe haven for them.

As we pray, God will do miracles. I believe that the Lord is near to bring restoration to relationships, even to the most difficult and strained relationships.

Restoration of Godly Manhood

My husband's name is Sam. In physical and emotional strength, he is incredibly strong. He is grounded, stable and dependable. In our family, he takes the role of servant. He works diligently, and he works hard to provide. In recent conversations, I heard him tell another that "*being a husband and father is about being responsible; it is taking responsibility for his family. It is about stewarding these gifts well.*" In his role as leader, he is kind and patient and embodies the virtues of Jesus. Our family benefits from his strength of character.

My prayer for boys and men is that they will be free to embrace the unique ways that God has made them and that they will embrace their strength, courage, tenderness and love, all of the attributes of God.

My prayer is that God will restore men as kings and priests. Men are kingly in their personhood and in their stewardship to lead. Men are called to be priests who minister to the Lord and who minister to their families.

May God restore dignity to boys and men in the majesty of all that God has made them to be.

Restoration of Women

My prayer is that The Lord will restore women as daughters of the Lord, made in the image of God. My prayer is that women will understand their intrinsic value as children of God. My prayer is that God will open up the eyes of women to know the beauty and wisdom of God's ways. I pray that women will walk in the honor and dignity that God lavishes upon them. I pray that God will restore the gift of motherhood within our culture.

Balm of Gilead

For the hurt of the daughter of my people I am hurt. I am mourning; Astonishment has taken hold of me. Is there no balm in Gilead? Is there no physician there? Why then is there no recovery for the health of the daughter of my people? Jeremiah 8:21, 22 NKJV

The prophet Jeremiah mourns over the hurt of his people. My heart is broken over the wounds of the American family.

"Pay close attention to your tears," said prayer giant, Lou Engle, "what you weep over has to do with your destiny." If you weep over fatherlessness, over the orphan; if your heart is broken over those who are touched by any type of sin and brokenness, there, in that arena, may God use you to pray and to act.

•

The Christian community should send such a fragrance of Christ's love that the world will run to it. When they come to us, will we have the skills to be the physician that heals the soul?

Is there the balm of healing within us?

LESSONS IN PRAYER

First, God is not looking for eloquent prayers, rather He is looking for prayers from the heart. The Bible tells us that fervent prayers of the righteous accomplish much.

Pray from the heart. Pray simple prayers with the expectation that God hears and will answer. "I cry aloud to the LORD; I lift my voice to the LORD for mercy. I pour out my (prayers) before Him," David said in Psalm 142.

During these prayer times we will pray for the restoration of *the family unit* in America, as well as for families that you know.

Prayers for the Institution of the Family Unit

Father, we recognize that our only help is in You. We humble ourselves before you and ask for a move of Your Spirit. We pray from Malachi, that You will send the spirit of the prophet Elijah. We ask that You will turn the hearts of the fathers to their children, and the hearts of the children to their fathers.

Restore the family unit. Move in our nation. Open our eyes to see You. Help us to know that You are our only answer. We humbly seek You. We love you with all of our hearts. In Jesus Name. Amen.

Prayers for Men

Dear God, we ask for restoration of boys and men in America. We ask you, Father, to intervene in our nation, to bring restoration of honor to men.

We pray that the institution of fatherhood would be honored in communities, within the marketplace and in media.

Lord, we pray for men to be instilled with courage and confidence, gentleness, purity and patience. We ask for a supernatural wind to change the landscape of 'family' across our nation.

Prayers for Women

Father God, thank you that You are the Creator. You know the intrinsic value of the lives of women. Help us to return to You. Help us to have wisdom in how we might lead lives that are fulfilling and pleasing to You. Show us Your ways and teach us Your truth. Thank you for Your great grace.

Prayers for Marriages

Father, we pray for restoration of the institution of holy matrimony. We ask You for a renewed understanding of Your Ways. Pour out Your Grace, so that marriage will once again be honored in culture. Genesis 2:24.

Prayers for Sexual Purity

Father God, bring a renewed understanding that Your ways are higher than our ways. Restore sexual purity to our nation.

Prayers for Children

Father, we pray for America's children. Help us to grow in the knowledge of You. Show us Your light and Your truth, so that we might walk in Your ways. Aid us in the work of raising our children. Give us Your great grace. Where we have erred, forgive us and bring us back unto Yourself. Give wisdom where we lack.

Release our children into Your great grace. Heal wounds and restore. Raise up the greatest generation of lovers of God that the world has ever seen. Psalm 24:6 "This is the generation of those who seek Him, who seek Your face." NASB

Raise children who will step forward in Your restoration power. "Your people will volunteer freely in the day of Your Power: in holy array, from the womb of the dawn, Your youth are to You as the dew." Psalm 110:3 NASB

Help us, as parents, where we carry guilt and shame. Forgive us and heal us, as is Your desire. Restore our hearts. Thank you for Your great mercy and Your faithfulness. Thank you for your unconditional love for us.

Release prayers for healing of wounds in all people, related to breakdown of the family.

Prayers for Church Community

Father, make us the balm of Gilead. Help us to carry the comfort of the Holy Spirit.

We ask that You would move in the community of the Church. Bring fresh strategies for renewal for the family unit. Bring forth teachers who will draw Your people back to truth, with grace and love. Move in our families with Your love and Your power. Strengthen pastors to do Your Will. Bring back into focus the importance of strong family units. Grant us, as a society, healing from Your hand. Show us Your grace and Mercy. In Jesus Name.

Father, we lift up our educational systems in the United States. We ask for a change in our system. We ask for Your grace and wisdom for families; aid them in their choices. Help them to be the voice within their communities. Revive us again, we pray. In Jesus Name.

Some practical questions to ask yourself:

- Does my family have a set time each day where we turn off our devices and connect with one another?
- Does my family have any type of time around 'the hearth,' daily readings of and conversations about the Bible?
- Am I, as a parent, helping my child to connect with God through reading the Bible and seeking encounters with Jesus? Am I doing this at home?
- Recognizing that there are seasons in life, what is our family mission? What talents and dreams does each member of the family have, and how are we supporting these dreams? Are our dreams God-centered, intended to bring God glory?

- Are we connected to a local church? Do we give enough time to our church community? Do we also place a high value on developing our family's faith within our home?
- Does my family need to set boundaries? (Suggested reading material, *Boundaries* by Cloud & Townsend.)
- Do I need to learn new skills about marriage or parenting? Do I need a mentor? What intentional steps can I take to learn skills?

Arrow 3: Church Government

AIMING AT BELIEF

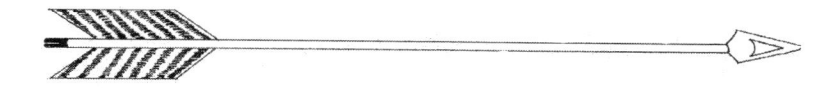

> *The Spirit of the Sovereign Lord is on me because the Lord has anointed me to proclaim good news to the poor. He has sent me to bind up the brokenhearted to proclaim freedom for the captives and release from darkness for the prisoners, to proclaim the year of the Lord's favor and the day of vengeance of our God, to comfort all who mourn, and provide for those who grieve in Zion—to bestow on them a crown of beauty instead of ashes, the oil of joy instead of mourning, and a garment of praise instead of a spirit of despair. They will be called oaks of righteousness, a planting of the Lord for the display of his splendor. They will rebuild the ancient ruins and restore the places long devastated; they will renew the ruined cities that have been devastated for generations.*
> Isaiah 61:1-4

Jesus defined his ministry when he first spoke in the temple, quoting the prophet Isaiah. Our ministries should reflect His priorities - the preaching of the Gospel, the restoration of the saints and the sending of these into the world to rebuild and restore culture.

As leaders in the Christianity community, we must examine our fruit. Here are some questions that can guide us on our journeys to honor God.

- Are we seeking, above all else, to know Him and to make Him known?
- Are we working to build healthy people within our ministries, and is this work effective?
- Are we prioritizing families, teens and children?
- Are we helping individuals to discover their individual talents and God's unique purpose for them?
- Are we imparting the necessary skills to our congregants, so that they might go into every sphere of influence as salt and light?
- Are we prioritizing and incorporating prayer into our gatherings? *"For my house will be called a house of prayer for all nations."* Isaiah 56:7, Matthew 21:13

Jesus cares so tenderly for those who shepherd the church. Jesus cares so tenderly for His Bride. I know that He wants to walk with us on our journeys, lift our burdens and bring us into greater fruitfulness.

I also believe that He wants to empower us afresh to reach the lost and to bring the wisdom of God into every sphere of culture.

Prayer Targets: Aiming at Belief within the church.
- Prayers for your pastors and church leaders.
- Prayers that the church will function as it should in order to bring the Gospel to our cities and to the world.
- Prayers that individuals will take the responsibility for their own faith walk.

First, pray for and support the pastors and leaders at our churches and for the churches in our cities.

> *The elders who direct the affairs of the church well are worthy of double honor, especially those whose work is preaching and teaching.*
> 1 Timothy 5:17

Having walked the path of senior and associate pastors for many years, I am well acquainted with the unique sacrifices that pastors and their families make in order to follow Jesus into the roles of leadership to which He calls. The pressures to hear and follow God and to provide leadership to a congregation can be overwhelming.

The statistics for the welfare of the American pastor are pretty grim. Depression and stress levels are extremely high among pastors. The statistics about pastor's lives and families are compelling:

- "72% of the pastors report working between 55 to 75 hours per week.
- 84% of pastors feel they are on call 24/7.
- 80% believe pastoral ministry has negatively affected their families.

- 78% of pastors report having their vacation and personal time interrupted with ministry duties or expectations.
- 65% of pastors feel they have not taken enough vacation time with their family over the last 5 years."[47]

Many pastors succumb to burn out.

Believers can support their pastors in many ways, but one of those ways is to actively and consistently pray for them and for their families.

When I think of my current pastor, they are full of life and continually allow God to pour out His refreshing on them! It is possible for leaders to continue in His grace and to run the race that is set before them with endurance. We have a role to play.

Pray from the book of Ephesians, chapter 1. Ask the Lord to continually draw pastors into intimacy and the knowledge of Jesus. Pray for wisdom and hope.

> *For this reason, ever since I heard about your faith in the Lord Jesus and your love for all the saints, have not stopped giving thanks for you, remembering you in my prayers, in order that the God of our Lord Jesus Christ, the glorious Father, may give you a spirit of wisdom and revelation in your knowledge of Him. I ask that the eyes of your heart may be enlightened, so that you may know the hope of His calling, the riches of His glorious inheritance in the saints, and the surpassing greatness of His power to us who believe.*
> Ephesians 1:15-19

From Ephesians 3, pray that pastors and their families would experience God's love for them.

> *For this reason, I bow my knees before the Father, from whom every family in heaven and on earth derives its name. I ask that out of the riches of His glory He may strengthen you with power through His Spirit in your inner being, so that Christ may dwell in your hearts through faith. Then you, being rooted and grounded in love, will have power, together with all the saints, to comprehend the length and width and height and depth of His love, and to know the love of Christ that surpasses knowledge, that you may be filled with all the fullness of God.*
> Ephesians 3:14-19

As ministers of the Gospel, "*enable your servants to speak your word with great boldness*" Acts 4:29. We pray for our pastors that they will be filled with the Fire of God and strengthened to stand as pillars of righteousness in a dark time.

We pray:
- for God's continual grace
- for Grace and Peace to be multiplied
- for rest for the soul and body
- for strategies to enjoy a Sabbath rest, for patterns of prioritized time with family
- for blessed marriages, blessing on children
- for abundant Wisdom and Direction
- for faith to be increased

- for abundance of joy, peace and freedom
- for increased financial blessings, generosity of members and boards.

In my studies, I discovered this scripture, from Malachi 2:5-7. I think that it is a good exhortation to ministers, that they would live in reverence of God and preach the word of God in truth. In these verses, God spoke to the priests.

> *My covenant was with him, a covenant of life and peace, and I gave them to him; this called for reverence and he revered me and stood in awe of my name. True instruction was in his mouth and nothing false was found on his lips. He walked with me in peace and uprightness, and turned many from sin. For the lips of a priest ought to preserve knowledge, because he is the messenger of the Lord Almighty and people seek instruction from his mouth.* Malachi 2:5-7

Prayers

Father, we ask that ministers of the Gospel will live in reverence of You. We pray that they will preach the truths of Scripture. Deliver them from the fear of men. We cry out for Your grace and mercy. Let grace be multiplied to them.

Let the fire of God be upon them. Draw our ministers into a place of Awakening. Thank you for Your great mercy and love upon pastors and Christian leaders. Lead them in Thy Truth.

Turn Your Face towards ministers of the Gospel and bless them. Renew and refresh them. Lead them into all of truth and pour out Your abundant grace upon them. Strengthen their frames and make them like well-watered gardens, whose streams of water never fail. In Jesus Name. Amen.

For our second prayer target, pray that the church in America functions in such a way that members are equipped and empowered to fulfill the work of Christ.

The Bible puts a high value on the relationships that believers have with one another. *"Let us hold resolutely to the hope we profess, for He who promised is faithful. And let us consider how to spur one another on to love and good deeds,"* (Hebrews 10:23-24).

Furthermore, the book of Hebrews encourages us to be a part of a local work, *"let us not neglect meeting together, as some have made a habit, but let us encourage one another, and all the more as you see the Day approaching,"* (Hebrews 10:25).

When we gather together, we turn our attention and our affection to the Lord in worship, celebrating all that He is to us. A second purpose for the gathering of believers is so that Christians will be equipped and built up; then, from within the walls of church, believers should *go out* into every sphere of society. Religion is not intended to be a sphere of influence that is separate from other spheres (government, entertainment, media, education etc.); rather, people of faith are to be influential in all areas of life.

The Lord wants us to *"go and make disciples,"* (Matthew 28:18). So often when we read these words, we think of going into other nations, but we are also called to steward the cities in which we live.

Our cities have need of the transforming power of the Gospel. We must be those who answer the call to reach the poor, to serve in government, to support the police, to work in education and business - to be salt and light in all areas of culture. There, we should embody Christ. Beyond that, *we are called to bring the principles of scripture into every aspect of our businesses, into education, into government etc.*

We are going to pray that churches in the United States continue to grow in the knowledge and grace of the Lord, so that people are built up; so that the Gospel is preached; so that Christ receives glory.

God gives us a pattern for the functionality of 'church' in the book of Ephesians:

> *So Christ himself gave the apostles, the prophets, the evangelists, the pastors and teachers, to equip his people for works of service, so that the body of Christ may be built up until we all reach unity in the faith and in the knowledge of the Son of God and become mature, attaining to the whole measure of the fullness of Christ. Then we will no longer be infants, tossed back and forth by the waves, and blown here and there by every wind of teaching and by the cunning and craftiness of people in their deceitful scheming. Instead, speaking the truth in love, we will grow to become in every respect the mature body of him who is the head, that is, Christ. From him the whole body, joined and held together by every supporting ligament, grows and builds itself up in love, as each part does its work.*
> Ephesians 4:11-16

It is my sense that the Lord wants to do a radical work in the churches of America. God wants to empower believers and send them into the communities where there are hurt and broken people who are in need of Him.

I sense an almost earthquake-like explosion of God's power in order to bring reform. My prayer is that we will hear and follow the gentle voice of the Lord and be in step with His will and His ways. My prayer is that we will embrace all that the Holy Spirit desires to do.

Consider harnessing the power of prayer within your congregation by inviting members to create prayer groups that focus on different aspects of culture. Our consistent prayers will garner God's attention and invite Him in- to work mightily in our cities and in our nation.

Prayers

Father, we pray for our church communities to embrace all that You want to do within them. We pray a special grace for our pastors. Expand our thinking, so that we might follow You more fully. Help us to know you in deeper ways.

Refresh and renew, we pray. Bring us into a yoke that is easy and a burden that is light. Bring Awakening to our Christian communities. Awaken across denominational lines.

Bring us into unity around the Scriptures. Let Your truth be preached in every pulpit. Bring Glory to Your Name. In Jesus Name, Amen.

Third, pray for believers- that we would be stewards of our own faith and respond to God's invitation into a deeper relationship with Him.

Knowing Christ

David Benner writes that, "any authentic spiritual journey must grow from direct, personal experience of God. There is no substitute for a genuine encounter with perfect love." He quotes Tozer, when he says, 'Knowledge by acquaintance is always better than knowledge by description.' Benner goes on to say that, "Knowing God is not simply a matter of believing certain things about him. Personal knowing goes beyond objective knowing."[48]

The personhood of the Lord, the many aspects of His nature - His love, knowledge, understanding and power - are vast beyond measure. He is not in the image of our making, but was and is and always will be in His own image. The Lord has so much that He wants to reveal to us.

Consider these and other scriptures that describe the nature of God. This scripture might be different from some of the usual ways that we describe Jesus. This scripture focuses on a Mighty God, a sovereign God. It focuses on God's Faithfulness. It describes His eyes that burn with the purity and passion of fire.

> *Then I saw heaven standing open, and there before me was a white horse. And its rider is called Faithful and True. With righteousness He judges and wages war. He has eyes like blazing fire, and many royal crowns on His head. He has a name written on Him that only He Himself knows...And from His mouth proceeds a sharp sword with which to strike*

down the nations, and He will rule them with an iron scepter.... And He has a name written on His robe and on His thigh: King Of Kings And Lord Of Lords.
Revelation 19: 11-16

As you meditate on these words, *and on other passages* in the Bible that describe the nature of God, may He continue to reveal Himself to you.

Second, as believers, we must look for our identity within the person of Christ. In order to fulfill God's plan for our lives, we must discover our unique talents and gifts, and we must steward them well. It is up to *each of us* to seek the Lord, so that we understand His will for us. Although the larger church has a role in assisting us along the path of our journey, we will be held accountable to God for our own faith, our own choices and the stewardship of our lives.

We are also responsible for the condition of our hearts. As the Bible says, "Get rid of all bitterness, rage and anger, brawling and slander, along with every form of malice. Be kind and compassionate to one another, forgiving each other, just as in Christ God forgave you." Ephesians 4:31, 32. It is the Lord's desire to heal our wounds and to restore our souls. His desire for us is that we live in health. 3 John 1:2 It is His desire that we live an abundant life. John 10:10

Prayers

Father, we pray for all believers to have encounters with Your love.

We ask You to remove barriers to faith; heal wounds and restore hearts. Isaiah 53:5, Psalm 147:2

Give great grace to all of Your sons and daughters. 2 Corinthians 9:8

Bring us into Your truth. Psalm 25: 5

Strengthen our faith. Luke 22:32, Jude 1:20, Ephesians 3:16

We ask for encounters with Your consuming fire. Hebrews 12:29

Show us Your Glory. Exodus 33:18-20

Send us into the world. Matthew 9: 38, Mark 16:15

As Isaiah said, we say, Here am I, send me!
Isaiah 6:8.

Therefore, since we are surrounded by such a great cloud of witnesses, let us throw off everything that hinders and the sin that so easily entangles. And let us run with perseverance the race marked out for us, fixing our eyes on Jesus, the pioneer and perfecter of faith. For the joy set before him he endured the cross, scorning its shame, and sat down at the right hand of the throne of God. Consider him who endured such opposition from sinners, so that you will not grow weary and lose heart.
Hebrews 12:1-3

Arrow 4: State and Local Governments

AIMING AT INTEGRITY

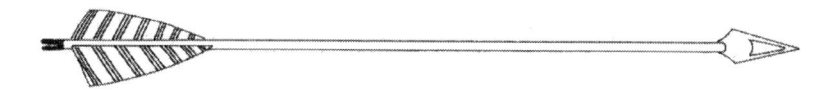

For this arrow, we will be covering two prayer targets. The first is to pray for your city and state. We will specifically pray for state and local representatives. Second, we will be discussing the power of an individual to affect different spheres of culture.

> **Seek the peace and prosperity of the city to which I have carried you into exile. Pray to the Lord for it, because if it prospers, you too will prosper.** Jeremiah 29:7

It is a sobering thought to realize that The Lord has given us stewardship over our towns and cities (Genesis 1, Joshua 1, Matthew 5:13-16, Matthew 28). In Jeremiah 29, we are commanded to *seek the peace and prosperity* of our cities. We are commanded to *pray for our cities*.

Pray for your city, for your government officials and police force. Pray for different aspects of your city.

Command the favor of God over your city. Pray for peace within your city.

LESSONS IN PRAYER

Petition: to make or present a formal request to (an authority) with respect to a particular cause.

Intercession: the action of intervening on behalf of another.

First of all, then, I urge that petitions, prayers, intercessions, and thanksgiving be offered on behalf of all men for kings and all those in authority.
1 Timothy 2:1-2

Seek the peace and prosperity of the city to which I have carried you into exile. Pray to the Lord for it, because if it prospers, you too will prosper.
Jeremiah 29:7

Thanksgiving:
In everything, by prayer and thanksgiving, let your requests be made known.
Philippians 4:6 NASB

Prayers for State and Local Leaders

I cannot emphasize enough how important your state and local governments are. The impact of these representatives on your life and the lives of your children is enormous. In this section, you will pray for state executives, lawmakers and judges. The decisions they make today will affect generations to come.

Included in this section is your local law enforcement, whom we honor as God's servants, for their self-sacrifice.

I have had the privilege of witnessing the hard work and dedication of many of our local leaders. Lift them in prayer, with gratitude for their service. I encourage you to research, write down the names of your appointed and elected state and local representatives, so that you can pray for them by name.

- Governor & Lt. Governor of your state
- State representatives, as a body
- Chief Justice of State Supreme Court (and Justices)
- Mayor of your city
- City Council, School Boards
- Chief of Police

Prayers

Father, we come before you with our petitions, asking for men and women to pursue service in government.

We ask You to speak to men and women to run for office, and we ask for obedience. Enlarge our courage and faith, that these servants can accomplish what might seem impossible.

We pray for godly elected officials. We ask You to raise up men and women, like Daniel, who will not bow their knees to ungodliness and will not succumb to unrighteousness.

Release Your emissaries into the earth. Release carriers of the Gospel into our local governments.

We ask for the saving grace of Jesus come to all of our representatives. Let revival begin in all of our states.

Please be a shield, a covering and protection to representatives, according to Psalm 91. Be a shield to them and their families and keep them from harm.

We pray for Supernatural wisdom; right decisions to be made.

Let Righteousness, Justice and Mercy be executed within our towns, cities and states.

We pray that the things that are hidden to be revealed. Expose corruption; let righteousness prevail.

We pray for Great Awakening in Governor's offices, State Offices, Mayoral offices and in Police Force. We pray Thy Kingdom come and Thy Will be done, in Jesus' Name. Amen.

THE POWER OF INTEGRITY

I have been thinking about the power of a life, about how one individual can make a difference in history. Keep this in mind when you think about your city. What can you contribute to its welfare?

Daniel's story is that of a life that was dedicated to the Lord. It is a story of *one man* who *changed the world by faith*. As I have studied the life of Daniel, I have been struck by his remarkable courage and integrity in the face of cultural opposition. Daniel interacted with *the most powerful men* of his age. As a captive in New Babylon, Daniel served under two Babylonian kings, Nebuchadnezzar and his son, Belshazzar. He also served under two Persian kings, Darius and Cyrus the Great. Daniel was a servant in the governmental realm for over seventy years. In addition to Daniel's incredible service as a governmental leader, his life provides a stellar example of a faithful and diligent intercessor. Daniel was God's secret weapon within a culture that did not know Him.

Daniel's life is the story of incredible courage and devotion to his faith. After surviving the year long siege of his city, Jerusalem, witnessing the effects of severe famine and bloodshed, Daniel, a teenager, was taken from his home to New Babylon. We can only imagine the fear, despair and loneliness that he must have experienced. Yet, Daniel refused to compromise his religious traditions and faith; he stood resolute against the pressures of overseers and authorities. He did not bow to the pagan culture that surrounded him.

God gave great favor to Daniel in the midst of his circumstances. His excellence, skill and knowledge took him to the highest levels of service under Nebuchadnezzar.

During his service to the king, Nebuchadnezzar had a troubling dream which none of his advisors or religious leaders could interpret. These religious men were put to death for their failure to interpret the king's dream. It was then that Daniel, upon the threat of death, came forward with the interpretation that provided the king with understanding of the dream. Recognizing that the God of the universe was upon Daniel,

> *King Nebuchadnezzar fell on his face, prostrate before Daniel, and commanded that they should present an offering and incense to him. The king answered Daniel, and said,* **"Truly your God is the God of gods, the Lord**

of kings, and a revealer of secrets, since you could reveal this secret." Then the king promoted Daniel and gave him many great gifts; and he made him ruler over the whole province of Babylon, and chief administrator over all the wise men of Babylon. Daniel 2:46-48 NKJV

This is an amazing example of the Providence of God over one young man's life. What an incredible example of the power of God! This ungodly and unrighteous king recognized- through the power of God in Daniel's life - that The Lord is God! What glory Daniel brought to the Lord through his humility, courage and obedience!

Later in Daniel's life, his service, knowledge and skills were so outstanding that King Darius considered making him the sole overseer of the kingdom, serving directly under the king. This was when the adversaries of Daniel, Haman in particular, sought to destroy Daniel by devising a plan that would be a direct assault upon Daniel's faith. Haman convinced King Darius to disallow prayers to any besides the king himself.

Daniel, in his faithfulness and integrity, because of his devotion to the Lord, continued his habit of prayers. He boldly prayed in the open, upon his porch for all to see, defying the king's order.

Only the Lord knows the nature of his prayers - but we can imagine that he prayed for courage and steadfastness for himself. He probably prayed for his friends, other Jewish captives. I believe that he prayed for his homeland, for Jerusalem. I believe that he wept over his city and cried out for its restoration.

Maybe he prayed that God would make His mark upon Babylon, that God would intervene, that God would raise up a leader like Cyrus who would release the Jews back to their homeland. Maybe he was the intercessor to whom God looked with favor in order to *bring about His will concerning the homeland of the Jews*. Certainly, he was the man to whom the Lord gave great insight and prophetic wisdom, not only for his age, but wisdom that speaks to us, thousands of years later! What faith! What steadfastness!

We know the extraordinary story of God's deliverance of Daniel from the wild beasts. What an amazing life and testimony - one that we still read to our children and grandchildren.

Never underestimate what God can do through a single man or woman of character. Sometimes history hinges on the contributions of *a single individual*. Throughout history, men like Constantine, who obeyed the vision he saw before the Battle at Milvian Bridge and, later, legalized the practice of Christianity throughout the Roman Empire; and Francis of Assisi, who served the poor and founded hospitals; John Wycliffe, Bible translator; Queen Margaret, the Pearl of Scotland, a woman given to prayer and charitable deeds; and men of great character, like George Washington, Father of our nation; William Wilberforce, who persisted in Parliament and wrote legislation that ended the slave trade in Britain; Abraham Lincoln, Winston Churchill - men who stood for liberty and saved nations; Mother Teresa who gave dignity to the least among us; these individuals, many with the flame of God in their bones, changed the course of history and impacted the world for good. Never underestimate what God can do with a life that is surrendered; with a life of service; with one life that is marked by great character.

Do not underestimate what God can do through your life!

My prayer is that the Lord will raise us up as people who unashamedly follow Jesus, whose lives, like Daniel's, are marked by integrity.

My prayer is that God will identify men and women who will sense that the purpose of their life is to go into specific areas of culture: government, education, media, business, with an understanding of mission. It is time for Christians to re-engage culture.

Be Bold and Take Action!

Daniel was a man who lived his life counter to the culture around him. God is looking for men and women who will be courageous enough to speak truth in a way that is counter to the prevailing culture that we see in America.

You are the voice that God will use as a spark to change the culture around you. He will fill your voice with power, as He did Daniel's.

- Dare to ask the Lord to use you and to display His power through you.
- Seek the Lord for a personal mission. Cry out as Isaiah did, "*Here am I, Lord; send me!*" Isaiah 6:8

Arrow 5: The Federal Government

AIMING AT ENDURANCE

"But what is government itself, but the greatest of all reflections on human nature?"
James Madison

"The condition upon which God hath given liberty to man is eternal vigilance; which condition if he break, servitude is at once the consequence of his crime and the punishment of his guilt."
John Philpot Curran

Overarching Questions:
1. What is the origin of our rights, and why does this matter?
2. What type of government best secures and protects personal liberties, equality and justice?
3. What keeps us from tyranny (cruel and oppressive governments)?
4. What happens in times of Constitutional Crisis?
5. What is the role of Christians in civil government?

George Orwell said that "The most effective way to destroy people is to deny and obliterate their own understanding of their history."

It is vital that we understand both the ideals and the form of our federal government, so that we will be informed and responsible citizens, indeed, so that we might steward this great nation, preserving it for future generations. If we hope to function in a world that is less politically polarized, then we must have a working knowledge of the Constitution, so that we have the ability to approach issues through the lens of the Constitution, rather than through our own personal biases. Doing this will safeguard our culture and protect our freedoms. In many ways, the following is a call to return to the first principles of our founding, governmental principles that, heretofore, have safeguarded our liberties. These laws have allowed for unprecedented religious, economic and social freedoms.

I encourage you to study history and our founding documents. Primary documents provide for us accurate historical facts, as well as the perspective of the founders.

The history of the founding of the United States is extraordinary. The succession of events, the assembly of men of genius and the unique time in the progression of history produced a revolution and a republic that sent shockwaves throughout the nations.

Much of the greatness of our nation is due to the fact that the overwhelming majority of our early citizens viewed the world through the lens of Judeo-Christian values and, in general terms, held to the morals of that worldview.

This excerpt about the importance of religion is from President George Washington's Farewell Address, 1796.

> "Of all the dispositions and habits which lead to political prosperity, religion and morality are indispensable supports. *In vain would that man claim the tribute of patriotism who should labor to subvert these great pillars of human happiness — these firmest props of the duties of men and citizens. The mere politician, equally with the pious man, ought to respect and to cherish them.* A volume could not trace all their connections with private and public felicity. Let it simply be asked, Where is the security for property, for reputation, for life, if the sense of religious obligation desert the oaths which are the instruments of investigation in courts of justice? *And let us with caution indulge the supposition that morality can be maintained without religion. Whatever may be conceded to the influence of refined education on minds of peculiar structure, reason and experience both forbid us to expect that national morality can prevail in exclusion of religious principle.*"[49]

The second contributor to the acceleration of prosperity and blessing on our nation is the fact that we have been tethered to our founding charters and to the rule of law. Our government was founded on *ideals*, set forth in the Declaration of Independence in 1776, and, in *form*, documented in the Constitution of the United States and Bill of Rights. These charters declare the origin of our liberties, define natural rights, explain the purpose of government, delineate assigned powers, separate powers and describe the rule of law.

The truths of the Declaration - the premise that the rights to life, liberty and the pursuit of happiness - spoke deeply, not only to the conscience of Americans, but to the peoples of the world. Deep within the hearts of men, they, like we, believed that men were accountable to God and were, by right of birth, free.

Third, although capitalism has its drawbacks, it is the fairest of all economic systems because in this capacity wealth is accumulated based on merit. The United States is not entirely a free market, capitalist society, but we still reap the benefits of our roots. Carmen Alexe, who grew up in communist-controlled Romania, wrote for the Foundation for Economic Freedom, stating that "only in a free market system can we truly achieve individual liberty and human flourishing," and that, "individual freedom can only exist in the context of free market capitalism." [50] If Americans continue to embrace socialists principles, if in fact we are not able to pull back from principles of socialism, there will be losses in social and religious freedoms.

In light of our current cultural wars, the prayers in this arrow aim at endurance, echoing the thoughts posed by Abraham Lincoln at the dedication of the National Cemetery of Gettysburg.

> "Our fathers brought forth on this continent, a new nation, conceived in Liberty, and dedicated to the proposition that all men are created equal. Now we are engaged in a great civil (cultural) war, testing

whether that nation, or any nation so conceived and so dedicated, can long endure."

THE UNITED STATES OF AMERICA

Nation: The word is used in English in a broad sense, "a race of people an aggregation of persons of the same ethnic family and speaking the same language," and also in the narrower sense, "a political society composed of a government and subjects or citizens and constituting a political unit; an organized community inhabiting a defined territory within which its sovereignty is exercised."[51]

In these definitions of nations, we see three main ideas. The first is the cultural idea of a family, united by language and common descent.

Second, nations are derived from ancestral roots and from these roots, political entities emerge. In this, the United States is unique as it is a melting pot of differing ethnic roots. Even so, as expressed in our national motto, *E Pluribus Unum*, unity is best preserved by assimilation.

Third, in stable nations, sovereignty is exercised over a defined territory.

Civil Government is defined as "the system of polity in a state; that form of fundamental rules and principles by which a nation or state is governed."[52]

Principles of Civil Government, as understood in Scripture:
From *God and Government, A Biblical and Historical Study*
by Gary DeMar

1. "All power is ordained by God and the state is one such power. Man's law must be rooted in God's law; lawlessness, in this sense is resistance to God. First of all, civil government is of divine institution. It is ordained by God is a part of God's kingdom and government" (Romans 13:1-2).
2. Civil government is ordained to promote good by providing conditions for its welfare by punishing criminals and thus preventing crime. Its essential foundation is justice, godly order (Romans 13:3-4).
3. "Civil government has the approval of Christian conscience. It is an authority like that of parents and church officers which is ordained of God, the only rightful source of authority."- R.J. Rushdoony, *Politics of Guilt and Pity*

Why do we need civil governments?

"If men were angels, no government would be necessary. If angels were to govern men, neither external nor internal controls on government would be necessary." Madison, Federalist Paper #51

Government is a social contract, a voluntary contract by a group (nation) in which men agree on laws for the common good that protect all citizens, rather than for the few. Government exists to protect the natural rights of all citizens. Government is instituted to 'promote good by providing conditions for its welfare by punishing criminals, thereby, preventing crime.'[53]

Forms of Civil Government:

The following is quoted from *God and Government, A Biblical and Historical Study,* by Gary DeMar.

"Anarchy – Anti-government. The individual is a rule unto himself. There is no higher law, whether it be another man's or god's, that he is obligated to keep. In reality, he is his own god. Modern day terrorism is anarchist in its nature.

Autocracy – the absolute rule by a monarch or dictator. The individual in power is uncontrolled and has unlimited authority. The people have no way to resist him, except by force.

Bureaucracy – The rule or manipulation of a people by non-elected officials and civil servants. A bureaucracy can make laws independent of any system of law.

Communism -The total control of state and society by a single, non-elected authoritarian group or party where the individual exists to serve the state. Control of all aspects of society is by force. Communists advocate the abolition of all forms of religion; the destruction of private property and the abolition of inheritance; absolute social and racial equality; destruction of all forms of representative or democratic governments, including civil liberties such as freedom of speech, freedom of the press, and of assemblage.

Goals of Communism, from *The Communist Manifesto.*
1. Abolition of property in land.
2. A heavy progressive or graduated income tax.
3. Abolition of all right of inheritance.

4. Confiscation of all property of all emigrants and rebels.
5. Centralization of credit in the hands of the State, by means of a National bank, with State capital and an exclusive monopoly.
6. Centralization of the means of communication and transport in the hands of the State.
7. Other combinations of manufacturing industries under State control.
8. Free education for children in public schools."

Democracy – Government directly by the people with rule by the majority. This is the law of majority opinion, "the dictatorship of the 51%" (Francis Schaeffer). Absolutes are found in the will of the people, not in God's eternal laws. Democracy is a government of the masses."[54]

"Constitutional government is defined by the existence of a constitution—which may be a legal instrument or merely a set of fixed norms or principles generally accepted as the fundamental law of the polity—that effectively controls the exercise of political power."[55]

Our Constitutional Republic is defined as "Government through elected representatives. It is the privilege and duty to elect representatives. Checks and balances are in place, including the division of power between federal and state governments. A document is written, in the form of a covenant or constitution, and is the means by which a system of law is implemented."[56]

> "Humanity has won its battle; liberty now has a country," declared the Marquis de Lafayette, so unique was the formation of United States as it burst upon the world.

America's Founding

It is almost impossible for modern Americans, who daily enjoy the security and liberties of our nation, to understand the world in which the peoples of the earth lived at the time of our founding.

It was a world without electricity, a world without advanced forms of transportation and communication.

It was also a world where kings ruled without restraint, where the rule of law was *almost* non-existent. With few exceptions, human rights were *completely disregarded*. Since the time of the ancients until the signing of the Magna Carta in 1215, the *concept* of human rights was absent from political thought. It was not until the late 17th century that the rights of life and liberty were beginning to be addressed.

In addition, in most communities, the threat of invasion by marauding enemies was a daily threat. Communities did not enjoy peace and stability.

Pre-Columbian life expectancy in area of Southern United States was 25 to 30 years.[57] "17th-century English life expectancy was only about 35 years, largely because infant and child mortality remained high. Life expectancy was under 25 years in the early Colony of Virginia, and in seventeenth-century New England, about 40 percent died before reaching adulthood."[58]

Upon this backdrop, our founders articulated the enduring principles of natural rights and wrote the U.S. Constitution, the longest lasting and most enduring constitution in history. The United States was exceptional in its founding, as well as in the history of mankind. It is a form of government that is worthy of our defense.

THE MARCH OF HISTORY

THE ANCIENTS

Our founders looked to the government of the Ancient Hebrew people, as well as to classical civilizations of Greece and Rome as examples. These are the civilizations that Thomas Jefferson and others studied intently as models of civil government. (Educated in law, history, philosophy and the study of the ancients, Jefferson spoke five different languages and read Latin and Greek.)

ENGLAND LEADS THE WAY

Magna Carta. Signed in the year 1215, by King John, 'The Great Charter', is one of the most important documents in history as it established "the principle that everyone is subject to the law**,** even the king, and guarantees the rights of individuals, the right to justice and the right to a fair trial." Although not uniformly enforced, this great charter paved the way for principles of liberty.[59]

Parliament. The Magna Carta provided the preliminary steps towards the establishment of a representative governing body for the English. The form and character of Parliament has changed throughout the centuries. By the 17th and 18th centuries, Parliament worked with the Monarch in the rule of Britain.

English Bill of Rights. Signed in 1689 by William III and Mary II, the English Bill of Rights is landmark legislation that set the stage for a Constitutional monarchy and outlined freedoms for English citizens. Some of the freedoms outlined in the English Bill of Rights were the freedom to elect members of Parliament and the freedom to speak within Parliament.[60]

Enlightenment Philosophers: Many say that John Locke had an influence on the content of the English Bill of Rights, with his proposal of the natural rights of citizens.

Philosophers in Europe began to ponder the function of government during the Enlightenment Period of the late 1600 through 1700s. Men like Charles Montesquieu, John Locke and others wrote significant treatises on the ideals and mechanics of government.

THE FOUNDING OF THE AMERICAS:
AN EXCEPTIONAL HISTORY

A HISTORY OF SELF-GOVERNMENT

By April 19, 1775, when shots were fired that began America's war with Britain, the colonists had practiced a form of self-government for one hundred and fifty years.

In 1619, at the Jamestown Settlement, Virginians selected their first representatives and named this body, The House of Burgesses. The Pilgrims of Massachusetts functioned, at first, under the Mayflower Compact. Other colonies developed representative bodies under governorships and charters.

Isolated as the Americas were from Europe, separated by the Atlantic Ocean, the colonists were British citizens who functioned under local, colonial representative governments as well as under

British appointed governorships. On the whole, the colonists functioned in their daily lives without much interference from England, operating under the practice of British salutary neglect. During this period, the colonists began to tackle cultural questions, political and religious issues, some of which would be later stated in the Declaration of Independence.

It was not until the conclusion of the French and Indian War, in 1763, that England began to enforce taxes, such as the Sugar Act, Tea Act, Stamp Act, which were burdensome to the colonists.

By the time of the Revolution, in practical terms, the colonists were concerned with their lack of representation within Parliament, as well as with the growing interference of the king in matters that concerned the colonists. These matters dealt with the idea of the consent of the governed. In theoretical terms, the colonists were increasingly convinced of the principles of their rights to equality.

Even after battles were fought in Massachusetts, American leaders sought reconciliation with Britain. For almost a year, battles were fought around Boston, and the city was placed under siege. By March of 1776, when the colonists defeated the British in the Battle of Dorchester Heights, the British armies retreated from New England and were gathering on Long Island, New York with the intent of capturing New York City.

The Declaration of Independence

In 1776, the Continental Congress, meeting in Philadelphia, assigned to five men the task of writing a declaration.

The purposes of the declaration were to dissolve the bonds of government between Britain and the American colonies and to clearly state the reasons for this dissolution.

Beyond this, the profound purpose of the Declaration was to proclaim the enduring natural rights for which our founders were willing to give their lives.

The theory of natural rights was a part of American thought from the 1760s forward. Natural rights are enduring rights, given to all men *by God*. The founders considered these rights to be *inherent rights for all men given to man by the Creator. These rights are true for all, appropriate to all times. These rights are fixed and enduring.* It was a revolutionary idea to believe that all men are born with rights, given to them by their Creator, as opposed to being granted by a king or by government. This is vital to understand. If rights are given to us by God, then government exists to protect these rights. If rights are given to us by the government- the right to life and liberty- then government can take away rights when it suits the government to do so.

The idea that men are created "equally free and independent was a radical idea in the history of political thought."[61] The understanding that the power to govern comes from the consent of the governed was also a revolutionary, radical idea.

In light of these concepts, Thomas Jefferson penned these words, "We hold these truths to be self-evident, that all men are created equal, that they are endowed by their Creator with certain unalienable rights, that among these are life, liberty and the pursuit of happiness. That to secure these rights, governments are instituted among men, deriving their just powers from the consent of the governed."[62] These are 'Final Causes,' principles for which one would give up one's life.

Governmental Principles: Natural Rights

- All men are created equal.
- Unalienable rights to life, liberty and the pursuit of happiness are given to us by God.
- Governments are established among men for the purpose of securing rights.
- The just power of government comes from the consent of the governed.[63]

The Declaration went on to describe twenty-seven grievances (communicated previously and often) which the colonists believed were violations by King George III and Parliament.

Following the grievances was the declaration of dissolution between the colonies and the British Crown, a declaration of their dependence upon God and the pledge of their fortunes, their honor and their lives to these principles.

"We, therefore, the representatives of the United [64] States of America, in General Congress, assembled, appealing to the Supreme Judge of the world for the rectitude of our intentions, do, in the name, and by the authority of the good people of these colonies, solemnly publish and declare, that these united colonies are, and of right ought to be free and independent states; that they are absolved from all allegiance to the British Crown, and that all political connection between them and the state of Great Britain, is and ought to be totally dissolved…… **For the support of this declaration, with a firm reliance on the protection of Divine Providence, we mutually pledge to each other our lives, our fortunes and our sacred honor."**[65]

An Exceptional Revolution

For five more years, American soldiers suffered and died as they battled for the principles of liberty. The fact that the Americans were able to outlast and often outmaneuver the British, who were more numerous, better equipped and better trained is a testament to the steadfastness, fortitude and bravery of the American generals, men like George Washington, Henry Knox, Nathaniel Greene, and Daniel Morgan. Many would attribute America's victories to the hand of Providence.

Considering the challenges that the Colonial Armies faced, the American victory was nothing short of miraculous. By October 19, 1781, the British suffered their final defeat and surrendered at Yorktown, Virginia. The Treaty of Paris was signed in September of 1783. The last of the British troops left New York City in September of the same year.

The Greatest Character of the Age

On December 23, 1783, George Washington resigned his post as Commander-in-Chief. "Happy in the confirmation of our Independence and Sovereignty, and pleased with the opportunity afforded the United States of becoming a respectable Nation, I resign with satisfaction the Appointment I accepted with diffidence.

I consider it an indispensable duty to close this last solemn act of my Official life, by commending the Interests of our dearest Country to the protection of Almighty God, and those who have the superintendence of them, to his holy keeping."[66]

So radical was the resignation of the commander of a victorious army that King George III praised George Washington with these words: "that act closing and finishing what had gone before and viewed in connection with it, places him in a light **the most distinguished of any man living**, and that he thought him **the greatest character of the age.**" [67]

Articles of Confederation: A Weak Federal Government

From 1783 until 1787 the United States functioned under the Articles of Confederation, so wary were the colonists of forming a strong central government. This Confederation lacked any Executive Branch or Presidency (the Executive would later be created by the U.S. Constitution). The government, under these articles, proved itself too weak to deal with issues, such as local uprisings, tax collection and the national debt.

One success during the Confederacy was the addition of the Northwest Territories to the original colonies. It is significant that the national leaders were able to add these territories where, by law, slavery would not be extended. These territories would be added as states: Ohio, Indiana, Illinois, Michigan, Wisconsin and Minnesota.

During this time, men wrestled with the ideas of civil government. What kind of government best protected the rights of its citizens? By 1787, fifty-five representatives met in Philadelphia in an attempt to conquer the tremendous challenge of forming a government that could be agreed upon by the states.

THE CONSTITUTION OF THE UNITED STATES OF AMERICA: AN EXTRAORDINARY AND EXCEPTIONAL GATHERING OF MEN

What occurred in Philadelphia during summer of 1787 was an intersection of men and the Divine. The most brilliant men, studious and industrious, with knowledge of all forms of governments, came together with the goal of forming a more perfect union. William Gladstone was right when he described the U.S. Constitution as "the most wonderful work ever struck off at a given time by the brain and purpose of man.[68]

Upon the completion of the U.S. Constitution, Alexander Hamilton said, "For my own part, I sincerely esteem it a system which without the finger of God [Luke 11:20] never could have been suggested and agreed upon by such a diversity of interests."[69]

James Madison agreed, and reported: "It is impossible for the man of pious reflection not to perceive in it the finger of that Almighty Hand which has been so frequently and signally extended to our relief in the critical stages of the Revolution."[70]

Whereas the Declaration of Independence outlined Final Causes, the Constitution outlined "Formal Clauses," detailed descriptions of the form of government.[71]

It is important to understand that our form of government is not a democracy, rather it is a democratic republic, or representative government. James Madison wrote, "Pure democracies have ever been spectacles of turbulence and contention; have ever been found incompatible with personal security, or the rights of property; and have, in general, been as short in their lives as they have been violent in their deaths" (Federalist 10, 1).

Plato, (*The Republic*) informs us that, "tyranny arises, as a rule, from democracy." It is important that we watch both our language and the language of our representatives.

"The Constitution of the United States of America is the supreme law of the United States. Empowered with the sovereign authority of the people by the framers and the consent of the legislatures of the states, it is the source of all government powers, and also provides important limitations on the government that protect the fundamental rights of United States citizens."[72]

The reader is encouraged to read and study the Constitution of the United States.

Purpose of Constitution, from Preamble:
- "Ordained and established by We the People.
- Provided a more perfect union.
- Designed to provide equal justice for all.
- Designed to ensure peace, security, and domestic tranquility among the people.
- Provide for common defense against all enemies
- Designed the practices and policies which shall be for the general welfare of the whole nation

- To secure the blessings of liberty and prosperity for themselves and for their posterity."[73]

James Madison explained the challenge of creating a government that would *adequately rule over the governed* and *also control itself*. "In framing a government which is to be administered by men over men, the great difficulty lies in this: you must first enable the government to control the governed; and in the next place oblige it to control itself.

A dependence on the people is, no doubt, the primary control on the government; but experience has taught mankind the necessity of auxiliary precautions."[74] Madison looked to the people to be the primary controllers over government, but knew the necessity of laws (the Constitution) to support a control of the government. The Constitution was written in great measure to control and limit the power of government over the people.

Dr. Larry P. Arnn of Hillsdale College concludes that "government, therefore, should be energetic (have the strength to protect its citizens), but it should be limited."[75]

At the Constitutional Convention, many questions needed to be answered; many challenges awaited the representatives.

"Those particulars included such devices as representation, bicameralism, independent courts of law, and the "regular distribution of powers into distinct departments," as Hamilton put it in The Federalist No. 9; these were **"means, and powerful means, by which the excellencies of republican government may be retained and its imperfections lessened or avoided."**

Separation of Powers

Central to their institutional scheme was the principle of separation of powers. As Madison bluntly put it in The Federalist No. 47, the "preservation of liberty requires that the three great departments of power should be separate and distinct."

The founders believed that "The *accumulation of all powers*, legislative, executive, and judiciary, *in the same hands*, whether of one, a few, or many, and whether hereditary, self-appointed or elective, *may justly be pronounced the very definition of tyranny*." [76]

The separation of powers allows for checks and balances, so that no one branch becomes too powerful. For example: Veto power of the Executive Branch or judicial review by the courts. The separation of powers might be the most significant contribution of the Constitution to liberty for all men; for the preservation of our liberties and as an example for the nations of the world.

The Separation of Powers within the Federal government:
1. Legislative Branch-Makes the laws.
2. Executive Branch-Enforces the laws.
3. Judicial Branch-interprets the laws.

Key Elements of the Constitution

Popular Sovereignty: power comes from the people. "This reflects the mandate of the Declaration of Independence and is the recognition that the ultimate authority of a legitimate government depends on the consent of a free people."[77]

The establishment of Federalism – Division of power between states and national government "The institutional design was to divide sovereignty between two different levels of political entities, the nation and the states. This would prevent an unhealthy concentration of power in a single government. It would provide, as Madison said in The Federalist No. 51, a "double security . . . to the rights of the people." Federalism, along with separation of powers, the Framers thought, would be the basic principled matrix of American constitutional liberty."[78]

The Constitution delineates powers given to the federal government and the powers given to the state. "Federal government dealt with foreign policy, as well as regulation of harmony of the states in commercial regulations to create a national free market etc. States functioned in domestic policy. States were expected to protect property, contracts, family, moral education and common education."[79]

1. Delegated powers-held by federal government.
2. Reserved Powers-held by states.
3. Concurrent powers-given to federal government, without barring the same powers from the states, as in establishing a court system, taxation.

During the Constitutional Convention, many compromises were made that dealt with representation of the states in Congress. The Congress adopted the Connecticut Compromise and the 2/3 Compromise.

The U.S. Constitution was signed by thirty-nine who were in attendance and then required the ratification of at least nine of the thirteen states.

As a safe-guard against a central government that would be too strong, the Anti-Federalists demanded that a Bill of Rights be adopted. The first ten amendments to the Constitution were proposed in 1789 and approved in 1791. There are currently 27 Amendments to the U.S. Constitution.

NOTE: For a more detailed understanding of the roles and duties of each branch of the federal government, as well as a copy of the Bill of Rights, see Addendums One and Two at the end of the book.

The rights defined in the U.S. Constitution were revolutionary and continue to be precious, dear, worthy of defense. We are stewards of our nation and have the responsibility of participation in this sphere of government- through the vote, in political discourse, by making our voices heard. Our civil government receives its power by the consent of the governed.

Scriptural References for Prayers for Rulers:

First of all, then, I urge that entreaties and prayers, petitions and thanksgivings, be made on behalf of all men, for kings and all who are in authority. 1 Timothy 2:1-2 NASB

We are compelled by scripture to pray for rulers and for those who are in authority.

The Greek word 'PROTOS' is translated to English as "first of all" and means-principal, first, of primary importance. The next phrase, "I urge" comes from the word the 'PARAKALO' meaning to send for, summon, invite, exhort or admonish.

First of all, then, I urge that entreaties and prayers, petitions and thanksgivings, be made on behalf of all men, for kings and all who are in authority. 1 Timothy 2:1-2

The Apostle Paul is imparting principles to his son in the Lord. Paul highlights the importance of praying for governmental leaders and clearly admonishes Timothy to remember to pray for rulers and those who are in authority.

(Pray) *so that we may lead a tranquil and quiet life in all godliness and dignity.* 1 Timothy 2:2

Do not miss here that Paul emphasizes that prayers for rulers benefit those who are under the ruling authorities, "so that we might live a tranquil and quiet life in all godliness and dignity." We pray for the blessing and salvation of our rulers, but *it is to our benefit* that we pray, so that our families, our children and grandchildren might continue to live, free from government oppression. If Paul admonished those under Roman authority to pray, how much more so should we who live in a free society, in a republic in which power is derived from its people, pray for our rulers.

> *First of all, then, I urge that entreaties and prayers, petitions and thanksgivings, be made on behalf of all men, for kings and all who are in authority. This is good and acceptable in*

the sight of God our Savior, who desires all men to be saved and to come to the knowledge of the truth.
1 Timothy 2:1-4

These prayers please God our Savior.

These prayers create an atmosphere that is conducive to the preaching of the Gospel. They support freedom of thought and speech, so that men might hear the Gospel and come to the knowledge of the truth.

Prayers of thanksgiving and blessing for our federal government is our minimal sacrifice to God in this sphere.

Praying for the Executive, Legislative and Judicial Branches of Government

For this arrow, our aim is endurance. We ask you to pray for civil government at the federal or national level. Pray for revival to truth. Pray for stability and endurance. Pray God's will be done. Pray for protection. Pray for the winds of Awakening and supernatural intervention.

Prayers for the Executive Branch

We pray that Your kingdom comes within the White House. May your power and glory be made known to the President and his/her family; to the Vice President and his/her family. Bring them to the saving knowledge of Jesus Christ.

Father, please protect the office of the President. Let Your eyes be upon our President. Place Your Hand upon him/her for good.

We pray that our President would be an instrument of righteousness.

We pray that Your righteous judgments are made known. We ask for divine wisdom to be granted to the President and to every member of the cabinet. May they make decisions that are aligned with the principles of scripture. Intervene where there is not righteousness and justice and prudence.

Lead our Executive to stand for life, liberty and freedom. Uphold religious freedom in our land. Protect the rights that are set forth in the Constitution. Protect rights to freedom of worship and freedom of speech.

Let Your hand be on the President for his/ her good.

Shield and protect the inhabitants and the employees of the White House, as well as those who enter there. According to Psalm 91 protect the Executive.
Lord, turn your face towards the city of Washington, D.C. Forgive our sins and heal our land. Show us your mercy and your grace. We give You thanks and praise!

Protect our nation. Protect the rule of law. Protect the integrity of our federal government. In the Name of Jesus.

We plead the blood of Jesus over the Executive.

(Include your prayers for the President of the United States)

Prayers for the Legislative Branch

Father, we humbly come before You and ask for Your mercy and Your grace.

First, give Americans an understanding of our rights to elect our representatives. We ask that you would break off apathy; stir your people to understand the great freedoms that we enjoy. Aid us in your understanding. Give us your wisdom and guide us as we participate in civil government.

We pray for our elected officials in the Senate. We ask that our Senators would be confronted with Your truth and awakened to reverence for You. Send Your power; Send your ministers of truth. Bring awakening to the Senate. We pray the same for the Representatives in the U.S. House. Send awakening.

Lord, refresh the souls and protect the lives of men and women who stand for righteousness.

Help our governmental servants to be examples of honesty and integrity. Aid them in making wise decisions. Turn their hearts away from selfish gain.

Expose corruption. Tear down all that exalts itself against Your Name. Bring humility and the fear of the Lord to Washington D.C.

Make us a city that shines with Your purity. Aid us, we pray. In Jesus Name, Amen.

Prayers for the Judicial Branch

The Supreme Court of the United States

Chief Justice John Roberts; Justice Clarence Thomas; Justice Ruth Bader Ginsburg; Justice Stephen Breyer; Justice Samuel Alito; Justice Sonia Sotomayor; Justice Elena Kagan; Justice Neil Gorsuch; Justice Brett Kavanaugh.

(Please edit as judges are replaced by others)

Prayers

Father, enable these servants of Yours to be instruments of justice and righteousness. Give them strength and ability beyond what they are able. Help them to withstand the assault of the enemy. Grant them wisdom in every decision. Guide the thoughts of our justices. Assist them in upholding righteousness and justice. Remind them of the Ten Commandments that adorn the walls. Open each heart to Your love and truth.

Let your wisdom prevail. Let Your truths be heralded through the decisions of the highest court in our land. Let Your righteous judgments rule. Intervene on the behalf of the righteous.

Fill vacancies with God-fearing Christian men and women. In Jesus Name, we pray. Amen.

To those who take an active role in government, we say thank you! Our prayers of gratitude, empowerment and protection are with you.

.

LESSONS IN PRAYER

Our fight is against spiritual forces in heavenly places. Finally, be strong in the Lord and in his mighty power. Put on the full armor of God, so that you can take your stand against the devil's schemes. For our struggle is not against flesh and blood, but against the rulers, against the authorities, against the powers of this dark world and against the spiritual forces of evil in the heavenly realms. Therefore, put on the full armor of God, so that when the day of evil comes, you may be able to stand your ground, and after you have done everything, to stand. Stand firm then, with the belt of truth buckled around your waist, with the breastplate of righteousness in place, and with your feet fitted with the readiness that comes from the gospel of peace. In addition to all this, take up the shield of faith, with which you can extinguish all the flaming arrows of the evil one. Take the helmet of salvation and the sword of the Spirit, which is the word of God. And pray in the Spirit on all occasions with all kinds of prayers and requests. With this in mind, be alert and always keep on praying for all the Lord's people.
Ephesians 6:10-18

Let's go a little deeper in our understanding of how prayer works. Let's study these words from the book of Daniel.

Daniel was seeking the Lord over the welfare of the Hebrew people. He decided to humble himself, to pray and fast. As he did this, he confessed the sins of his people.

A Fight in the Heavenlies:

> *"In those days I, Daniel, was mourning for three full weeks. I ate no rich food, no meat or wine entered my mouth, and I did not anoint myself with oil until the three weeks were completed. On the twenty-fourth day of the first month, as I was standing on the bank of the great river, the Tigris, I lifted up my eyes, and behold, there was a certain man dressed in linen, with a belt of fine gold from Uphaz around his waist. His body was like beryl, his face like the brilliance of lightning, his eyes like flaming torches, his arms and legs like the gleam of polished bronze, and his voice like the sound of a multitude. Only I, Daniel, saw the vision; the men with me did not see it, but a great terror fell upon them, and they ran and hid themselves. So I was left alone, gazing at this great vision. No strength remained in me; my face grew deathly pale, and I was powerless. I heard the sound of his words, and as I listened, I fell into a deep sleep, with my face to the ground. Suddenly, a hand touched me and set me trembling on my hands and knees. He said to me, "Daniel, you are a man who is highly precious. Consider carefully the*

words that I am about to say to you. Stand up, for I have now been sent to you. And when he had said this to me, I stood up trembling. "Do not be afraid, Daniel," he said, "for from the first day that you purposed to understand and to humble yourself before your God, your words were heard, and I have come in response to them. However, the prince of the kingdom of Persia opposed me for twenty-one days. Then Michael, one of the chief princes, came to help me, for I had been left there with the kings of Persia. Now I have come to explain to you what will happen to your people."
Daniel 10:2-14

When we pray, over cultural issues, there is a fight that occurs in the heavens. Even now, worldliness and worldly ways- pride, selfishness, lust and greed- fight in the heavenlies against the angels of God. Andrew Murray said, "We must begin to believe that God, in the mystery of prayer, has entrusted us with a force that can move the heavenly world, and can bring its power down to earth."

INTERCESSION

To intercede: the act of using your influence to make someone in authority forgive someone else or save them from punishment. As those who are in right standing with the Lord by the blood of Jesus, we are called to stand before God and make intercession on behalf of others. Often, intercession requires more time and is marked by fervent prayers.

Consider a Daniel fast to go along with your prayers and petitions. You can research the Daniel fast on the web for more information.

- When you pray, ask the Lord to fight against enemies of righteousness and freedom.
- Pray against apathy amongst the righteous.
- Pray against fear.
- Pray against false ideologies, false gods.
- Pray against idolatry.
- Pray against hatred and dissension.
- Pray against selfish ambition and greed.

Prayers

Father, we ask You to rid our nation of corruption and deception. Expose darkness. We ask that your ministering angels would fight for liberty, righteousness and justice in our nation at the highest levels. Bring forth your light and your truth. Break up the enemies of the Gospel. Send your truth, aid us with Your might.
May the voice of the Lord thunder over His enemies!

Pray Scripture

Contend, Lord, with those who contend with me; fight against those who fight against me. Take up shield and armor; arise and come to my aid. Brandish spear and javelin against those who pursue me.
Psalm 35:1-3

The voice of the Lord is over the waters; the God of glory (El Hakabodh) thunders, the Lord thunders over the mighty waters.
Psalm 29:3

(Refer to Adams and Lincoln's Declarations for Days of Prayers and Fasting as a prompt for prayer.)

Remember David's prayers; pray Psalm 18.

We pray that Your word prevails. Let Righteousness be exalted in our land again.

Prayers for Elections

Let the name of God be blessed forever and ever, for wisdom and power belong to Him. It is He who changes the times and the epochs; He removes kings and establishes kings.
Daniel 2: 20-21

Father, in our elections, we pray Thy will be done. We ask that You rule in the affairs of men. Give us just and wise leadership. Show our nation mercy. Lead us in the everlasting ways of truth. Allow our nation leaders who continue to support religious freedom, so that we might rear our children in the fear of the Lord, so that men might be saved and come to the knowledge of the truth. Let Your kingdom come in our government and Your will be done. Let righteousness and truth prevail. In Jesus Name, we pray.

Prayers for a Nation in Crisis

Heavenly Father, we confess our need and dependence upon You. At this time, we humble ourselves and appeal to Your mercy. Remember, Oh Lord, the faith of our fathers, and indeed, our faith. Remember our prayers and intercession. Hear, now, our faith, as we put our trust in You alone.

We stand before You with thanksgiving for every day that we have lived in freedom. Forgive us for forgetting You, for turning away and for serving other gods. Have mercy on us and cleanse our hearts and souls of the love of fame, pride, fortune; of lusts of the flesh and of desires for things other than You.

Forgive us for going our own ways, for not seeking You as we ought.

Lord, have mercy on us, in our ignorance and pride. Please forgive us our sins and bring us back to You.

For the sake of our families, for the sake of Your Son Jesus, forgive us and have mercy upon us. Against You only have we sinned. Blot out our sins and our transgressions and lead us in the everlasting ways.

In judgment, remember mercy. It is in Jesus Name we pray. Amen.

CONSTITUTIONAL CRISES

For expertise in the area, I have included materials from Hillsdale College Lectures, specifically, "The History and Meaning of the Constitution"[80]

The Constitution was tested under the administration of President Andrew Jackson in the implementation of tariffs. It was tested again in 1841, when President Harrison died in office. Provisions for who would serve in the event of the death of the president had not been included in the Constitution; therefore, the legitimacy of President Tyler's administration was in question. (This was solved in 1967 with the 25th Amendment.)

The most significant crisis to the Constitution occurred when states seceded in 1861. The issues of state secession and slavery were decided by the American Civil War.

During this time, **Abraham Lincoln affirmed his belief in principles of enduring natural rights**, when he wrote, "All honor to Jefferson--to the man who, in the concrete pressure of a struggle for national independence by a single people, had the coolness, forecast, and capacity to introduce into a merely revolutionary document, **an abstract truth, applicable to all men and all times, and so to embalm it there, that to-day, and in all coming days, it shall be a rebuke and a stumbling-block to the very harbingers of re-appearing tyranny and oppression.**"[81]

Many would argue that the next Constitutional crisis was introduced by the body of thought embraced by Progressives-Theodore Roosevelt, Woodrow Wilson and, later, by Franklin Delano Roosevelt. While Progressives were trying to combat issues of the Industrial Revolution, they broke with the traditional understanding of the natural rights of Jefferson, Locke and others. Progressives held a "critical, philosophic and fundamental difference" from Jefferson and Lincoln. -Dr. Ronald Pestritto, Dean of the Van Andel Graduate School of Statesmanship and Professor of Politics[82]

"This theory (Progressivism) held that the principles of the American Founding, expressed most eloquently and concisely in the Declaration of Independence, were irrelevant to modern life. *Progressives taught that stringent restrictions on government power were no longer necessary to protect liberty, since human nature and science had advanced greatly during the 19th century.* Progressives did not believe that individuals are endowed with inalienable rights by a Creator; rather, they believed that rights are determined by social expediency and bestowed by the government."[83] -Dr. Ronald Pestritto

Leading intellectuals like Frank Goodnow and John Dewey held progressive views. Frank Goodnow wrote, "The rights which he possesses are, it is believed, conferred upon him, *not by his Creator, but rather by the society to which he belongs.* What they are is to be determined by the legislative authority in view of the needs of that society. Social expediency, rather than natural right, is thus to determine the sphere of individual freedom of action" (Goodnow from *The American Conception of Liberty*).

President Wilson stated, "The trouble with the (natural rights) theory is that government is not a machine, but a living thing. It falls, not under the theory of the universe, but under the theory of organic life. It is accountable to Darwin, not to Newton. It is modified by its environment" (Wilson from *What is Progress?*).

Wilson pushed back against the ideas of checks and balances in government, leaning much more heavily on bureaucracies to administer government, rather than on three branches.

When social expediency dictates rights, who then sets the boundaries? Consider the following excerpt by Dr. Ronald J. Pestritto and Charles and Lucia Shipley, Hillsdale College Lectures: The Meaning and History of the Constitution. *The Progressive Rejection of the Founding*.

> "Whereas the Founders cautioned against direct democracy as subject to the whimsical passions of men to the detriment of reason, the Progressives embraced direct democracy. The internal arrangements of the Constitution—especially separation of powers—were established by the Founders to check the passions and encourage the rule of reason. However, they forestalled efficient and responsible government, according to the Progressives. Thus, government must be freed from the constraints of institutional checks in order to be efficient and truly responsive to the will of the people. While Wilson sought to make politics more democratic, the administration of government became less democratic. Wilson argued that separating politics from government by unelected experts would best accomplish the ends of

government. The Progressives thus fashioned the bureaucratic regulatory state—also known as the "administrative state." They believed that unelected and highly trained experts could govern the nation more rationally, effectively, and responsibly than mere politicians, who were often corrupt and beholden to voters. This further required that the President be understood as the national leader. The modern Presidency is an essential tool for the Progressive transformation of government. According to the Founders' understanding of the executive branch, the President's duties centered on national defense and the veto power. Wilson argued that the President, as the embodiment of national popular opinion, would be a singular force for the common good, able to lead the nation, including the two other branches of government, *through the force of his own will.* As the future President Wilson wrote, "His office is anything he has the sagacity and force" to do." [84]

While the founders understood that government would change, they believed that natural rights provide the bedrock for our government and that protecting those rights is the purpose of government. These rights, the rights to life, liberty and property are enduring rights for all people, at all times.

Prior to Wilson, Theodore Roosevelt introduced a plenary view of government- that government had the general powers to do what it needed to do. *Progressives generally share the common view that government at every level should be actively involved in bringing reforms.*[85] Continuing on, the Progressive view of government was the basis for President Johnson's Great Society.

The Progressive view of government is a divergence from the intention of the founders. Much of our current trillion-dollar debt, (a grave threat to our national security) can be traced back to the principles of Progressivism. I believe that many of the answers to our governmental problems lie also in a 'Return,' in a return to first principles.

RIGHTS TO PROPERTY

Franklin Roosevelt continued policies of the Progressives. "Franklin Roosevelt …often argued publicly that the Founders did not understand property rights to be as important as other individual rights. A reading of the important founding documents, however, shows clearly that the Founders held property rights to be as important as other human rights. In fact, at times they insisted that the right to acquire and possess private property was in some ways the most important of individual rights."[86]

"The moment the idea is admitted into society that property is not as sacred as the laws of God, and that there is not a force of law and public justice to protect it, anarchy and tyranny commence."[87]
John Adams *A Defense of the Constitutions of the Government of the United States of America*, 1787

"Government is instituted to protect property of every sort; as well that which lies in the various rights of individuals, as that which the term particularly expresses. This being the end of government, that alone is a just government which impartially secures to every man whatever is his own."[88] James Madison, Essay on Property, 1792

"A wise and frugal government, which shall leave men free to regulate their own pursuits of industry and improvement, and shall not take from the mouth of labor the bread it has earned — this is the sum of good government."[89] -Thomas Jefferson, First Inaugural Address, 1801

"Progressives in the twentieth century have in large part aimed at turning the American people away from their traditional attachment to property rights."[90]- David Upham

My concern is that Americans are naïve about the true impacts of progressive policies and socialism. Carmen Alexe, writing for the Foundation for Economic Education, states that "Capitalism advances private property; directs allocation of resources through supply and demand; attracts capital; and helps people be better people." She also states that "individual freedom can only exist in the context of free markets."[91]

Thomas Gordon, in his article, "Why Socialism Often Leads to Tyranny," states, "The siren song of socialism and communism is alluring. Perhaps it is human nature that we want to be taken care of in all circumstances and be assured that no other person has material circumstances much better than our own. But the record is crystal clear. Socialism and Communism lead to underperforming economies, loss of individual opportunity for generations, equality implemented by everyone being poor except the party of 'apparatchiks,' lack of innovation and progress, and incredible political and religious oppression."[92]

For examples of the startling deprivations of people who live under Socialism and Communism, research the U.S.S.R., Cuba, China, Venezuela. One resource is Rand Paul's book, *The Case Against Socialism,* published in 2019.

•

Over the last one hundred years, two other competing views on the purpose of government have been introduced into the American framework. The first is that government exists to solve problems, to participate in every aspect of life and society. The second is that government exists to serve the well-being of the least among us, as opposed to protecting the rights of all citizens- Dr. Thomas G. West. The founders argued that the purpose of government is to protect natural rights, equally for all men.

Concerning impeachment

Because I am writing this book during a season of impeachment of the President of the United States by the United States Congress, I will address impeachment. I think what is most evident by the current impeachment process is that we are a nation that is deeply divided. In Washington's Farewell speech, 1796, the President warned against factions or the development of political parties.

As explained by historians from the Mount Vernon Library, "In the early republic, most condemned parties as divisive, disruptive, and the tools of demagogues seeking power. "Factionalism," as contemporaries called it, encouraged the electorate to vote based on party loyalty rather than the common good.

Washington feared that partisanship would lead to a "spirit of revenge" in which party men would not govern for the good of the people, but only to obtain and maintain their grip on power. As a result, he warned Americans to guard against would-be despots who would use parties as "potent engines…to subvert the power of the people and to usurp for themselves the reins of government."[93]

Currently, there is a bitter divide seen in our citizenry and reflected in our representatives. The roots of these division are regional, cultural, educational and often related to worldview.

Our first steps toward restoration are to pray and seek the Lord for His wisdom and grace.

The second steps are to for us to be informed.

Third, we must actively and diligently participate in civil discourse and in civil government.

Prayers for Peace

Lord in our zeal for righteousness, make us instruments of your peace. Aid all Americans in our participation of civil discourse. Help us to return to civility. Help us to communicate, not attack. Be with all Americans as we seek You in order to find Your wisdom. Show all your mercy and your grace. Thank you for your love for every individual. Be our aid and our guard. Give us Your peace. In Jesus Name, Amen.

Cynicism: the result of a concerted effort

High school and college students of the last few generations have been mis-taught by educators as many teachers were influenced by the writings of Howard Zinn, author of *A People's History of the United States*. Howard Zinn who described himself as "something of an anarchist, something of a socialist. Maybe a democratic socialist," enflamed ideas of class warfare and emphasized racial tensions in our nation.

When asked, "How do you blend anarchism, socialism and communism," Zinn answered, "I'd like to think of taking the best elements of all of them."[94]

In August of 2019, Mary Grabar published *Debunking Howard Zinn: Exposing the Fake History That Turned a Generation against America*. Dr. Harvey Klehr, Professor Emeritus of Politics and History at Emory University and author of *The Communist Experience in America*, endorsed this book writing, "Mary Grabar has produced a devastating analysis of the lies, plagiarism, violation of academic standards and simpleminded-platitudes that characterize Howard Zinn's bestselling book, *A People's History of the United States*. That Zinn is taken seriously as a historian is sad commentary on the teachers who rely on his fantasies and a terrible disservice to the students who are forced to read it. And, as Grabar demonstrates, it has contributed to a serious and potentially disastrous misunderstanding of American history and society."[95]

While I was teaching standard and advanced placement U.S. History courses, I became well acquainted with just how many educators include Zinn's work in their classrooms, and it is across the board. The introduction of Zinn and others materials into our classrooms has produced a decidedly anti-American sentiment within many young people. It has also created fertile ground, in the minds of a generation, for the planting of socialism and communism. This can be seen in any of the current polling of younger generations.

A New Burst of Freedom; A Door of Hope

I believe that God is sending an Awakening to our nation. Along with this, my hope is that we can break through the current fad of cynicism and that a new sense of patriotism will arise in the hearts of Americans, a renewed appreciation and love for our country. In Webster's *1828 Dictionary*, he described patriotism as "Love of one's country; the passion which aims to serve one's country, either in defending it from invasion, or protecting its rights and maintaining its laws and institutions in vigor and purity."

Patriotism is not the same as nationalism. Patriotism, love of country, is similar to the love that you have for your family. Within families, within countries, there are problems that need to be solved. Sometimes, there is a lot of frustration and heartache, hard conversations that need to be had. But you stick with your family; you love your family. In a similar way, I hope that Americans will enjoy a renewed sense of love for America. All good things come from love; nothing good has ever come from hatred.

I keep thinking about Samuel Francis Smith's song, *My Country Tis of Thee*. This song of devotion was written during the 2nd Great Awakening that occurred from roughly 1820-1840. This was the time period that denominations like Methodists and Baptists grew quickly into prominence in the United States, as many thousands of people heard the preaching of the Gospel. Smith was a seminary student when he penned these words.

> "My country, 'tis of thee, Sweet land of liberty, Of thee I sing; Land where my fathers died, Land of the pilgrims' pride, From ev'ry mountainside, let freedom ring! Our fathers' God, to thee, Author of liberty, To thee we sing; Long may our land be bright, With freedom's holy light. Protect us by thy might, Great God, our King!"

Martin Luther King Jr. also chose the words of "My Country Tis of Thee" to use in his *I Have a Dream* speech. "Let Freedom ring!"

•

Thomas Jefferson said that no civilization can be both ignorant and free. It is so important that we understand our history. We must recognize and celebrate the positive contributions that the United States has made to the world. In the sphere of government, we must reason according to the Declaration of Independence and the U.S. Constitution, adopting a return to first principles.

Additionally, my prayer is that Christians will understand the stewardship that we have been given for our nation. We are called to be salt and light in every area of life. To love your nation, is not to idolize it, or to prioritize it above Kingdom life, but it is to bring kingdom principles into the sphere of government.

Prayers

Father, we humbly ask that You will lead us in the ways that are right. Break our apathy and fear; break off our disdain. Lead us in Your truth. Give us faith and courage to be Your voice to our culture. Purify us that we will represent You well. Give us aid as we humbly seek You. In Jesus' Name, Amen.

"It is rather for us to be here dedicated to the great task remaining before us -- that from these honored dead we take increased devotion to that cause for which they gave the last full measure of devotion -- that we here highly resolve that these dead shall not have died in vain -- that this nation, under God, shall have a new birth of freedom -- and that government of the people, by the people, for the people, shall not perish from the earth." Abraham Lincoln

Arrow 6: News & Media

AIMING AT TRUTHFULNESS

Media includes entertainment culture (movies, television shows and music), books, newspapers and news outlets. Warren Cole Smith, author of many books and Vice-President of *World Magazine*, said "the medium through which one views the world, affects thought and behavior." Think about the influence that the movies, television and music have upon our minds and upon our worldview. As Americans, our entertainment culture has a profound influence on our understanding of a wide variety of cultural issues. Smith talked about the profound impact that the telling of stories has on our lives. The topic of entertainment is not the focus of this book, but I do pray that Christians will gain influence in this tremendous sphere of influence. For the health of our children, Americans must demand change in the entertainment industry.

Because of the rapid increase in how quickly information is brought to us through the media and because of the tremendous influence that the news has in our lives, prayer for truthfulness in news media is our fifth arrow.

Most major news organizations in America are owned by one of 15 billionaires. These include Michael Bloomberg, Bloomberg Media; Rupert Murdoch, NewsCorp, Fox News; Donald and Samuel Newhouse owners of Advance Publications with outlets like *Vanity*

Fair and *The New Yorker*; Cox Family which owns *Atlanta Constitution*; Jeff Bezos with *Washington Post*; John Henry with *Boston Globe*. [96]Please pray as God leads you for these and other owners of major media in the United States.

SHIFTS IN JOURNALISM

Not too many years ago, the job of a journalist was to report facts. Journalists took pride in maintaining integrity and self-restraint, reporting the facts without personal bias. Journalism has moved from objective, to interpretive and now to formulative in terms of disseminating information to the public. In large measure, journalists have been replaced by panelists who discuss everything from celebrities, to cooking, to fashion, and politics. In most cases, the practice of true journalism, one that holds to a consistent standard of ethics, is lost in our society. Aysha Taryam put it this way, "One might think it common sense, but in the world of journalism a lot of what makes sense is lost to the lure of favoritism, greed and fame. Sadly, in this truth-telling business, truth is hard to find."

At a recent seminar where Warren Cole Smith was the featured speaker, he talked about biases in media in the following terms. (The bullet points are from his work; the commentary is my own.)

- Framing- what goes into a story- reporting, photographs, statistics -and what is left out. Criss Jami said that, "Just because something isn't a lie does not mean that it isn't deceptive….one who speaks mere portions of truth in order to deceive is a craftsman of destruction."
- Including a limited or altered perspective in reporting

- Appropriation of language. 'Journalists' choose words, phrases and language that lead the consumer towards a particular conclusion. How language is used has a tremendous and lasting impact on our thinking.
- Ignoring spiritual influences in situations[97]
- A post-modern world where truth is 'relative, contextual and subjective.'

In today's media landscape, it is challenging to find news that is not reported from a particular political point of view. Consumers must be more diligent to find writers who consider objectivity a high value and who strive to report truthfully. Consumers of news media must be discerning in their consumption.

Furthermore, many of our main news sources in print and television now serve primarily as propaganda machines for our political parties. Our current media outlets seem to be purposefully orchestrating narratives on cultural and political issues. The effects of this are incredibly dangerous. "Freedom of the press can never be the license to say anything one desires. Freedom of the press is not the freedom to slander and attack and must never be used to fight other people's wars. It does not mean manipulating a story into speaking your views." Aysha Taryam

For more information on this subject, you might start by reading *Prodigal Press: Confronting the Anti-Christian Bias of the American News Media*, Revised and Expanded by Marvin Olasky, Warren Cole Smith.

An Anti-Christian Bias

Recently, I participated in a prayer call with Intercessors for America. I found it remarkable that the topic was Aiming at Truth in Media, just what I had chosen for the topic and aim of this arrow. On this particular call was a former technician from a major social media site. In his job as a technician, Eric Cochran began to research the coding against hate speech that was imbedded into this site. According to his testimony, as he looked, words like Christian, Bible verses, as well as pro-life language were causing the pages of certain persons to be deleted. Later, he found that certain conservative contributors were being blackballed from the site. Cochran resigned from his job and has since taken a job with Project Veritas, whose mission is to "investigate and expose corruption, dishonesty, self-dealing, waste, fraud, and other misconduct in both public and private institutions in order to achieve a more ethical and transparent society." Recently, Cochran was honored with an Impact Award for "going public and exposing Pinterest's agenda to censor pro-life content and Bible verses."[98] This is just one example of bias against Christian beliefs in media. Cochran is currently working with other whistleblowers in order to expose biases against Christian beliefs in media.

This sphere of influence needs a dramatic overhaul. Our prayers put a foot in the door in order to bring Christ into the situation, in order to say, 'no more to the enemy' and to declare the reign of Jesus. God can move mightily in this arena and bring transformation and restoration to truth in journalism.

Some prayer targets might include:
- Sweeping revival amongst current journalists
- Educational institutions that strive to teach objectivity in reporting
- Individuals who will stand up for truth within news organizations
- Christians to have a passion, burden and opportunities within the sphere of journalism

LESSONS IN PRAYER

Then the Lord reached out his hand and touched my mouth and said to me, "I have put my words in your mouth. See, today I appoint you over nations and kingdoms to uproot and tear down, to destroy and overthrow, to build and to plant. Jeremiah 1: 9-10

The book of Jeremiah, chapter 1, tells us that 'in our mouths is the power to tear down; to uproot; to destroy and to overthrow." There is a lot that has been sown into American culture that needs to be uprooted.

God went on to tell Jeremiah that by the word of his mouth, that he would also "build and plant." With our words (and actions) we can rebuild righteousness and love.

Prayers

Father, we come before You humbly, seeking Your will and Your ways. We pray for a fear of the Lord to be upon all members of the media. Please extend your grace to them. Draw them unto Yourself. Draw men and women back to the integrity of right principles of reporting. Help us, as the public, to hold media accountable to fact seeking and to telling the truth. Help us, Lord. Deliver us from lying lips.

Use the following scriptures to pray aloud.

Send out Your light and Your truth; let them lead us.
Psalm 43:3 NASB

For there is nothing hidden that will not be disclosed, and nothing concealed that will not be known or brought out into the open.
Luke 8:17

Pray for Bold and courageous reporters, who love truth.

Pray for freedom in the press.
Pray for an Awakening within the sphere of media.
Pray that reporters would love truth and righteousness.
Pray for protection of the freedom of the press.

Pray for Educators of Journalists to return to foundations of integrity in the press.

Arrow 7: The Preaching of the Gospel

AIMING AT AWAKENING

THE STORY OF PENTECOST

On the cross, Jesus suffered and died, exhibiting the ultimate expression of love for His Father and for us.

The cross of Jesus Christ and His subsequent resurrection is the great turning point in the history of mankind. It is the answer to the sins of the first Adam. Jesus' redemptive blood is the most powerful force in the earth, able to cleanse us from the deepest, darkest sins. His blood bought our redemption and our salvation.

After the death and resurrection of Christ, Jesus appeared to his disciples and to over five hundred people. *"He appeared to them over a period of forty days and spoke about the kingdom of God.*

On one occasion, while he was eating with them, he gave them this command: "Do not leave Jerusalem, but wait for the gift my Father promised, which you have heard me speak about. For John baptized with water, but in a few days, you will be baptized with the Holy Spirit." Acts 1:3-5

"But you will receive power when the Holy Spirit comes on you; and you will be my witnesses in Jerusalem, and in all Judea and Samaria, and to the ends of the earth." Acts 1:8

"After he said this, he was taken up before their very eyes, and a cloud hid him from their sight." Acts 1:9

In obedience to Jesus' instructions, the disciples gathered, hiding in an upper room, unsure of what would come. They prayed, and they remained. *"Suddenly a sound like the blowing of a violent wind came from heaven and filled the whole house where they were sitting. They saw what seemed to be tongues of fire that separated and came to rest on each of them."* Acts 2:2-3

This wind was the Holy Spirit.

This fire was also the Holy Spirit.

People around them thought that the disciples were drunk.

In the midst of this scene, Peter stood up to explain the outpouring of the Holy Spirit, referencing Old Testament scriptures. He went on to preach, *"Repent and be baptized, every one of you, in the name of Jesus Christ for the forgiveness of your sins. And you will receive the gift of the Holy Spirit. The promise is for you and your children and for all who are far off—for all whom the Lord our God will call."*

With many other words he warned them; and he pleaded with them, "Save yourselves from this corrupt generation." Those who accepted his message were baptized, and about three thousand were added to their number that day." Acts 2:38-41

•

Three things occur to me as I think about this story. The first, and most obvious thing, is that the disciples were gathered together and they were praying. The disciples earnestly sought God. They waited for the Lord to fulfill His words to them.

Indeed, Dr. Ronnie Floyd, wrote that, "There is no great movement of God that has ever occurred that does not begin with the extraordinary prayer of God's people."

The second thing that occurs to me is that the disciples had no idea what to expect concerning what was going to happen to or through them. Jesus told them that they would receive the Holy Spirit, that they would receive power, but they had no prior grid for the signs and wonders they experienced. They did not know that a mighty wind would come. They did not know to expect tongues of fire on their heads. And most surprising of all, they did not expect to speak in other tongues. The scene was so chaotic that those who viewed them said that they must be drunk. Some seemed to understand, but many did not.

The third thing that occurs to me is that God brought about His intended results; His goodness was experienced by those who listened and believed. He showed His glory; He kissed earth. He used the voices of men to change the hearts, and the world was set on fire.

REVIVALS THROUGHOUT HISTORY

Subsequent revivals and awakenings have similar markings to the day of Pentecost. The Great Reformation was marked by chaotic scenes. Men and women were tried in courts, burned at the stake, tortured, brutalized and murdered for refusing to compromise on their beliefs. During the years of the Reformation, God slowly and patiently revealed truth to men in ways that revolutionized our understanding of the Gospel. Translators began to write the Bible in native tongues, so that it could be read by people other than clergy. The printing press was improved upon, came into use and the Gospel spread to many nations. This burst of innovation in media changed the world.

In our own American history, we have experienced the First and Second Great Awakenings. During the First Great Awakening, under the preaching of Jonathan Edwards, men and women labored under the power of the Holy Spirit for days at a time, laboring to understand and receive the gift of salvation. People shrieked, wept and cried out for God's mercy. This must have been quite an untidy scene.

Up and down the East Coast, George Whitefield traveled, preaching in any place that would hold the large audiences who came to hear him speak. Often, he preached outside to crowds of thousands and tens of thousands. God used his extraordinary gifts of oration and amplification to preach to the masses. Whitefield was criticized for his dramatics and theatrics. Indeed, many of the religious people of his time rejected his message. Churches split over the message, and new churches were established. The First Great Awakening had a lasting impact on culture.

The Second Great Awakening was marked by even more fervor. Citizens from towns, villages and cities rode on horseback and traveled in wagons to meet under tents and out in the fields. These were the great Camp meetings. Circuit riders traveled from town to town bringing the good news of the Gospel. These meetings also brought the unexpected; these revivals were criticized and characterized by an emotional response to the Gospel. Men, women and children shook under the power of God. They wept and cried out to the Lord for forgiveness of their sins.

One thing is certain about revivals. When God's power is made known, men recognize their own sinfulness.

Henry Blackaby wrote that, "When Holy God draws near in true revival, people come under terrible conviction of sin. The outstanding feature of spiritual awakening has been the profound consciousness of the Presence and holiness of God." He also said, "During true revival, thousands of lost people are suddenly swept into the Kingdom of God. Scenes of the lost coming to the Savior in great, and unprecedented numbers, are common." God's goodness is revealed as He draws men, women and children to Himself and into communion with Him.

Many Americans are now praying for an Awakening. I believe that we must experience transformation in many areas of culture in order to survive and thrive as a society.

Revival revolves around the Gospel message, this beautiful good news that Holy Spirit brings.

All of these things were possible because of the cross.

> *Has not God made foolish the wisdom of the world? For since in the wisdom of God, the world through its wisdom did not know Him, God was pleased through the foolishness of what was preached to save those who believe. For the*

foolishness of God is wiser than man's wisdom, and the weakness of God is stronger than man's strength.
1 Corinthians 1:18-25

We are in many ways like those first, scared and lost disciples. We are desperate for God's faithfulness and mercy. We are calling on His character and goodness. We gain faith in Him, as we draw near.

But when we pray for Awakening, we do not know what the outworking of that will look like.

Just as many of the religious people during the time of the Reformation and of our Great Awakenings, rejected a move of God, we could miss what God is doing, unless we humble ourselves before Him.

Revivals do not fit well into our boxes. They do not mesh with our traditions. Often, our minds do not understand.

It takes courage to be a disciple. It takes courage to go to the cross. It takes even more courage to pick up our cross and to deny self. But, "there are no shortcuts that allow us to bypass the cross on the Christian spiritual journey," wrote David Benner.

As we cry out for Awakening, we may be surprised by its rumblings, by emotion, by signs and wonders.

If we respond…

Revival and awakening come, when and if God's people respond to Him. It is the principle of 2 Chronicles 7:14, *if my people, who are called by my name, will humble themselves and pray and seek my face and turn from their wicked ways, then I will hear from heaven, and I will forgive their sin and will heal their land.* I believe that this is true for America at this time. (In many other nations, there is currently a deep hunger and response to the Gospel.)

MARKED BY LOVE; MARKED BY POWER

As I said before, I believe that this new move of God will be marked by God's children encountering the love of God in fresh ways.

Here are some of my thoughts about signs that will mark awakening in our nation.

- People encountering the person of Jesus and His love.
- An increased capacity in the people of God to genuinely feel and move in compassion for others, to walk with the broken.
- Faith working through love (Galatians 5:6). Jesus did miracles when He was moved by compassion. When God's people are moved by the very compassion of God- when the compassion of heaven touches earth *through His people-* miracles will happen.
- Greater works will occur.
- New leaders emerging with supernatural wisdom and solutions to systemic problems.
- Inter-generational churches. Wherever churches can incorporate the older generation, a younger generation and the youngest generation of teens and children, gifts will be maximized; anointings will flow and increase.

- Emphasis in churches on building healthy people, healthy families. (Mission Community Church, Charlotte modeling this).
- Giftings in teens and children valued and incorporated into the larger church context, valued as a voice. Humility of the church reflected through this.
- Churches joining together to pray for their city or town. Walls that separate churches diminishing.
  Churches beginning to steward and care for their cities.
  People working together across denominational and ethnic lines. Unity in cities.
- Christians having the capacity to weep over sin. Christians awakened to the fact that they have offended God, sinned only against God, in a sense, hurt the very God of love.
- Whole cities, thousands coming to Christ in a move of power.
- Christians reaching marginalized people, walking with the hurt and the broken. Christians interacting with people outside of the church walls.
- Experiencing Power in Holy Communion as we remember Christ's death and resurrection.
- Heavenly fire (as in Pentecost) thrown upon the earth. God is a consuming fire that burns up chaff.
- Wonders. Things that bless, but that the mind cannot explain. Heavenly things on earth.

- Moves of God in people groups that had not heard the Gospel, including salvations and miracles
- Previously unreached people reached by missionaries
- Global (Supernatural) Fire
- Signs in the natural and then in the spiritual
- Supernatural Wisdom and solutions to systemic problems
- Occurrences that do not have a precedent.

The Lord might open up entirely new things that have not entered into the heart of man.

Pastor Ryan Carson at Mission Community Church has been teaching his congregation over the last years about embracing the mysteries of God's kingdom. He says that embracing mystery is often uncomfortable. It stretches us. And it allows us to be expanded, so that God might reside more fully within us, so that we might be His vessels to reach others.

•

The book of Revelation speaks of one such mystery when it talks about the prayers of the saints.

> *Another angel, who had a golden censer, came and stood at the altar. He was given much incense to offer, with the prayers of all God's people, on the golden altar in front of the throne. The smoke of the incense, together with the prayers of God's*

people, went up before God from the angel's hand.
Revelation 8:3-4

Our prayers rise as incense to God. They are cumulative in nature. They add up; they are not lost. Rather, they are held dearly by the Father.

Jesus told us that we should pray constantly and never give up. May our prayers rise as incense, as a pleasing sacrifice to God.

Our prayers are worship.

Prayers of Worship

There is no god like you and no works like yours. Lord, all the nations you have made will come and worship you. You are great and you do miracles. Only you are God.
Psalm 86:8-9 NASB

Oh come, let us worship and bow down; Let us kneel before the Lord our Maker. For He is our God, and we are the people of His pasture, And the sheep of His hand.
Psalm 95:6-7 NASB

Lord, take our hearts for Your own. Take our minds, will and emotions. Take our bodies as a reasonable and living sacrifice. Only You are God and worthy forever of our adoration and praise. Sweetest Jesus, our Savior, our Glorious King, we love you. Increase our love. In Your Name we pray.

Prayers for Mercy

The earth, O Lord, is full of Your mercy.
Psalm 119:64 NKJV

Great are Your tender mercies, O Lord.
Psalm 119:156 NKJV

The Lord is gracious and full of compassion. Great in mercy.
Psalm 145:8 NKJV

Prayers for Boldness

Pray also for me, that whenever I speak, words may be given me so that I will fearlessly make known the mystery of the gospel.
Ephesians 6:19

Pray that Christians will more boldly share the Gospel in every sphere of influence.

Prayers of the Blood of Jesus

We declare the Blood of Jesus over America that cleanses sin-disunity, perversion, corruption, greed, pride and lusts, in Jesus Name.

Prayers for Awakening in our Nation

Oh God, Show us Your favor. Forgive our iniquity. Cover all our sin.

Restore us again, God our Savior, and put away your displeasure toward us. Will you be angry with us forever? Will you prolong your anger through all generations? Will you not revive us again, that your people may rejoice in you? Show us your unfailing love, Lord, and grant us your salvation.
Psalm 85:4-7

Prayers for America

I pray, Lord; that Gospel will be preached with truth, and passion and conviction in all of the pulpits of America.

I pray that your Church will be a standard bearer to culture. Let us be a voice to America, light and salt to the world.

Father, may your kingdom values of righteousness, justice, mercy be exalted high above all others in our nation.

Even now, may Your Kingdom come and Your will be done, in Jesus Name.

We release the floodgates of heaven, the wave of God's Presence and Power that releases a supernatural Awakening to America. In Jesus Name.

Pray over the Scriptures of the preaching of the Gospel. Pray for an Awakening in our land. Ask the Lord of the Harvest to soften hearts and minds to the Gospel. Ask the Lord of the Harvest to send Workers into every sphere of our culture.

Prayers of Declaration Over Your City

Lift up your heads, you gates; be lifted up, you ancient doors, that the King of glory may come in. Who is this King of glory? The Lord strong and mighty, the Lord mighty in battle. Lift up your heads, you gates; lift them up, you ancient doors, that the King of glory may come in. Who is he, this King of glory? The Lord Almighty —he is the King of glory.
Psalm 24: 7-10

Will not God bring about justice for his chosen ones, who cry out to him day and night? Will he keep putting them off? I tell you, He will see that they get justice, and quickly. However, when the son of man comes, will he find faith on the earth?
Luke 18: 7-8

Final Thoughts

THE UPWARD CALL OF GOD

It is a time to whole-heartedly surrender to God's love and to the leading of the Holy Spirit. From this place of surrender, God can do through us greater than we have ever imagined. He will release upon the earth waves of salvation, restoration and hope.

"If with courage and joy we pour ourselves out for Him and for others for His sake, it is not possible to lose, in any final sense, anything worth keeping. We will lose ourselves and our selfishness. We will gain everything worth having." Elisabeth Elliot

May the words of the Apostle Paul be imprinted upon our hearts.

But whatever things were gain to me, those things I have counted as loss for the sake of Christ. More than that, I count all things to be loss in view of the surpassing value of knowing Christ Jesus my Lord, for whom I have suffered the loss of all things, and count them but rubbish so that I may gain Christ, and may be found in Him, not having a righteousness of my own derived from the Law, but that which is through faith in Christ, the righteousness which comes from God on the basis of faith, that I may know Him and the power of His resurrection and the fellowship of His sufferings, being conformed to His death; in order that I may attain to the resurrection from the dead. Not that I have already obtained it or have already become perfect, but I press on so that I may lay hold of that for which also I was laid hold of by Christ Jesus.

Brethren, I do not regard myself as having laid hold of it yet; but one thing I do: forgetting what lies behind and reaching forward to what lies ahead, I press on toward the goal for the prize of the upward call of God in Christ.

Philippians 3: 7-14 NASB

Addendum One

Explanation of the Purposes of the Executive, Legislative and Judicial Branches from the Constitution of the United States.

"Article One establishes the legislative branch of the federal government, the United States Congress. Under Article One, Congress is a bicameral legislature consisting of the House of Representatives and the Senate. Article One grants Congress various enumerated powers and the ability to pass laws "necessary and proper" to carry out those powers. Article One also establishes the procedures for passing a bill and places various limits on the powers of Congress and the states.

Article One's Vesting Clause grants all federal legislative power to Congress and establishes that Congress consists of the House of Representatives and the Senate.

Section 8 lays out the powers of Congress. It includes several enumerated powers, including the power to lay and collect taxes and tariffs for the "general welfare" of the United States, the power to borrow money, the power to regulate interstate and international commerce, the power to set naturalization laws, the power to coin and regulate money, the power to establish federal courts inferior to the Supreme Court, the power to raise and support military forces." U.S. Constitution.

Article Two of the United States Constitution establishes the executive branch of the federal government, which carries out and enforces federal laws. Article Two vests the power of the executive branch in the office of the president of the United States, lays out the procedures for electing and removing the president, and establishes the president's powers and responsibilities.

Section 1 of Article Two establishes the positions of the president and the vice president, and sets the term of both offices at four years. Section 1's Vesting Clause declares that the executive power of the federal government is vested in the president and, along with the Vesting Clauses of Article One and Article Three, establishes the separation of powers among the three branches of government.
Section 1 also establishes the Electoral College, the body charged with electing the president and the vice president.

Section 2 of Article Two lays out the powers of the presidency, establishing that the president serves as the commander-in-chief of the military and has the power to grant pardons and require the "principal officer" of any executive department to tender advice.

Though not required by Article Two, President George Washington organized the principal officers of the executive departments into the Cabinet, a practice that subsequent presidents have followed.

The Treaty Clause grants the president the power to enter into treaties with the approval of two-thirds of the Senate. The Appointments Clause grants the president the power to appoint judges and public officials subject to the advice and consent of the Senate, which in practice has meant that presidential appointees must be confirmed by a majority vote in the Senate. The Appointments Clause also establishes that Congress can, by law, allow the president, the courts, or the heads of departments to appoint "inferior officers" without requiring the advice and consent of the Senate. The final clause of Section 2 grants the president the power to make recess appointments to fill vacancies that occur when the Senate is in recess.

Section 3 of Article Two lays out the responsibilities of the president, granting the president the power to convene both houses of Congress, receive foreign representatives, and commission all federal officers. Section 3 requires the president to inform Congress of the "state of the union"; since 1913 this has taken the form of a speech referred to as the State of the Union.

The Recommendation Clause requires the president to recommend measures s/he deems "necessary and expedient." The Take Care Clause requires the president to obey and enforce all laws, though the president retains some discretion in interpreting the laws and determining how to enforce them.

Section 4 of Article Two establishes that the president and other officers can be removed from office through the impeachment process, which is further described in Article One.

Article Three of the United States Constitution establishes the judicial branch of the federal government. Under Article Three, the judicial branch consists of the Supreme Court of the United States, as well as lower courts created by Congress. Article Three empowers the courts to handle cases or controversies arising under federal law, as well as other enumerated areas. Article Three also defines treason.

Section 1 of Article Three vests the judicial power of the United States in the Supreme Court, as well as inferior courts established by Congress. Along with the Vesting Clauses of Article One and Article Two, Article

Three's Vesting Clause establishes the separation of powers between the three branches of government. Section 1 authorizes the creation of inferior courts, but does not require it; the first inferior federal courts were established shortly after the ratification of the Constitution with the Judiciary Act of 1789.

Section 1 also establishes that federal judges do not face term limits, and that an individual judge's salary may not be decreased. Article Three does not set the size of the Supreme Court or establish specific positions on the court, but Article One establishes the position of chief justice.

Section 2 of Article Three delineates federal judicial power. The Case or Controversy Clause restricts the judiciary's power to actual cases and controversies, meaning that federal judicial power does not extend to cases which are hypothetical, or which are proscribed due to standing, mootness, or ripeness issues.

Section 2 states that federal judiciary's power extends to cases arising under the Constitution, federal laws, federal treaties, controversies involving multiple states or foreign powers, and other enumerated areas. Section 2 gives the Supreme Court original jurisdiction when ambassadors, public officials, or the states are a party in the case, leaving the Supreme Court with appellate jurisdiction in all other areas to which the federal judiciary's jurisdiction extends."[99]

Articles Four through Seven:
These are: States and National Government; The Amendment Process; Supreme Law and other Provisions; Ratifying the Constitution (Articles of the Constitution).

Addendum Two

The Bill of Rights

Amendment I Congress shall make no law respecting an establishment of religion, or prohibiting the free exercise thereof; or abridging the freedom of speech, or of the press; or the right of the people peaceably to assemble, and to petition the Government for a redress of grievances.

Amendment II A well-regulated Militia, being necessary to the security of a free State, the right of the people to keep and bear Arms, shall not be infringed.

Amendment III No Soldier shall, in time of peace be quartered in any house, without the consent of the Owner, nor in time of war, but in a manner to be prescribed by law.

Amendment IV The right of the people to be secure in their persons, houses, papers, and effects, against unreasonable searches and seizures, shall not be violated, and no Warrants shall issue, but upon probable cause, supported by Oath or affirmation, and particularly describing the place to be searched, and the persons or things to be seized.

Amendment V No person shall be held to answer for a capital, or otherwise infamous crime, unless on a presentment or indictment of a Grand Jury, except in cases arising in the land or naval forces, or in the Militia, when in actual service in time of War or public danger; nor shall any person be subject for the same offence to be twice put in jeopardy of life or limb; nor shall be compelled in any criminal case to be a witness against himself, nor be deprived of life, liberty, or property, without due process of law; nor shall private property be taken for public use, without just compensation.

Amendment VI In all criminal prosecutions, the accused shall enjoy the right to a speedy and public trial, by an impartial jury of the State and district wherein the crime shall have been committed, which district shall have been previously ascertained by law, and to be informed of the nature and cause of the accusation; to be confronted with the witnesses against him; to have compulsory process for obtaining witnesses in his favor, and to have the Assistance of Counsel for his defense.

Amendment VII In suits at common law, where the value in controversy shall exceed twenty dollars, the right of trial by jury shall be preserved, and no fact tried by a jury, shall be otherwise reexamined in any Court of the United States, than according to the rules of the common law.

Amendment VIII Excessive bail shall not be required, nor excessive fines imposed, nor cruel and unusual punishments inflicted.

Amendment IX The enumeration in the Constitution, of certain rights, shall not be construed to deny or disparage others retained by the people.

Amendment X The powers not delegated to the United States by the Constitution, nor prohibited by it to the States, are reserved to the States respectively, or to the people.

"While the Bill of Rights created no deep challenge to federal authority, it did respond to the central Anti-Federalist fear that the Constitution would unleash an oppressive central government too distant from the people to be controlled.

By responding to this opposition and following through on the broadly expressed desire for amendments that emerged during the ratification process, the Bill of Rights helped to secure broad political support for the new national government. A first major domestic issue had been successfully resolved."[100]

End Notes

[1] Brown, Greg, et al. "Hebrew Year 5780 (2020): A Year to Widen Your Mouth in Wisdom or Zip It Shut." Sheerah Ministries, 29 Sept. 2019, sheerahministries.com/2019/07/03/hebrew-year-5780-2020-a-year-to-widen-your-mouth-in-wisdom-or-zip-it-shut/.

[2] Lexico, Oxford Dictionary.

[3] Monitor on Psychology, American Psychological Association, www.apa.org/monitor/2019/03/trends-suicide.

[4] "Drug War Statistics." Drug Policy Alliance, www.drugpolicy.org/issues/drug-war-statistics.

[5] "Transcript of President George Washington's Farewell Address (1796)." Our Documents - Transcript of President George Washington's Farewell Address (1796), www.ourdocuments.gov/doc.php?flash=false&doc=15&page=transcript.

[6] John Adams, October,1798

[7] 1. The Life and Writings of John Jay. The Review of the Life of John Jay. 1841.

[8] "James Madison and the Social Utility of Religion: Risks vs. Rewards." "James Madison and the Social Utility of Religion: Risks vs. Rewards," by James Hutson (James Madison: Philosopher and Practitioner of Liberal Democracy, A Symposium Held on March 16, 2001, at the Library of Congress), 16 Mar. 2001, www.loc.gov/loc/madison/hutson-paper.html.

[9] "The Finger of God on the Constitutional Convention." WallBuilders, 4 Apr. 2017, wallbuilders.com/finger-god-constitutional-convention/.

[10] Holy Bible: New American Standard. Broadman & Holman, 1993.

[11] https://virtueonline.org/seven-reasons-why-truth-matters-chuck-colson

[12] Ballard, Glenn. "The Real Heritage of Thanksgiving." Medium, Medium, 16 Jan. 2018, medium.com/@gcb1/the-real-heritage-of-thanksgiving-c1ca1acab0a

[13] Mulder, Cheryl. "Feasting and Fasting in Puritan New England." Collisions,28Nov.2016, amybeldingbrown.wordpress.com/2016/11/28/feasting-and-fasting-in-puritan-new-england/.

[14] Federer, William. "America Is a Nation That Called for Fasting and Prayer." The Washington Times, The Washington Times, 29 Nov. 2015, www.washingtontimes.com/news/2015/nov/29/power-of-prayer-america-is-a-nation-that-called-fo/

[15] Federer, William. "America Is a Nation That Called for Fasting and Prayer." The Washington Times, The Washington Times, 29 Nov. 2015,

www.washingtontimes.com/news/2015/nov/29/power-of-prayer-america-is-a-nation-that-called-fo/

[16] Federer, William. "America Is a Nation That Called for Fasting and Prayer." The Washington Times, The Washington Times, 29 Nov. 2015, www.washingtontimes.com/news/2015/nov/29/power-of-prayer-america-is-a-nation-that-called-fo/

[17] Federer, William. "America Is a Nation That Called for Fasting and Prayer." The Washington Times, The Washington Times, 29 Nov. 2015, www.washingtontimes.com/news/2015/nov/29/power-of-prayer-america-is-a-nation-that-called-fo/

[18] Federer, William. "America Is a Nation That Called for Fasting and Prayer." The Washington Times, The Washington Times, 29 Nov. 2015, www.washingtontimes.com/news/2015/nov/29/power-of-prayer-america-is-a-nation-that-called-fo/

[19] "March 23, 1798: Proclamation of Day of Fasting, Humiliation and Prayer." Miller Center, 23 Feb. 2017, millercenter.org/the-presidency/presidential-speeches/march-23-1798-proclamation-day-fasting-humiliation-and-prayer

[20] Abraham Lincoln's Proclamation Appointing a National Fast Day, www.abrahamlincolnonline.org/lincoln/speeches/fast.htm.

[21] Benner, David G. Surrender to Love: Discovering the Heart of Christian Spirituality. IVP Books, 2015.

[22] The Holy Bible: New King James Version. Thomas Nelson Publishing, 1985.

[23] Testament, Aphiemi In The New, and Aphiemi In TheSeptuagint. "Forgive/Forgiven - Aphiemi." Precept Austin, www.preceptaustin.org/forgive-aphiemi-greek-word-study.

[24] https://www.archives.gov/files/press/exhibits/dream-speech.pdf

[25] Love Your Enemies, sermons by Martin Luther King Jr.

[26] Elliot, Elisabeth. The Path of Loneliness: Finding Your Way through the Wilderness to God. Revell, 2007.

[27] DeMar, Gary. God and Government. American Vision Press, 2001

[28] Oxford Online Dictionary.

[29] Pearcey, Nancy. Love Thy Body: Answering Hard Questions about Life and Sexuality. Baker Books, 2019.

[30] https://plato.stanford.edu/entries/teleological-arguments/

[31] Pearcey, Nancy. Love Thy Body: Answering Hard Questions about Life and Sexuality. Baker Books, 2019.

[32] Benner, David G. Surrender to Love: Discovering the Heart of Christian Spirituality. IVP Books, 2015

[33] McInleyIrving.com

[34] Pearcey, Nancy. Love Thy Body: Answering Hard Questions about Life and Sexuality. Baker Books, 2019

[35] Pearcey, Nancy. Love Thy Body: Answering Hard Questions about Life and Sexuality. Baker Books, 2019

[36] Pearcey, Nancy. Love Thy Body: Answering Hard Questions about Life and Sexuality. Baker Books, 2019

[37] "Majority of Americans Now Believe in Cohabitation." Barna Group, www.barna.com/research/majority-of-americans-now-believe-in-cohabitation/.

[38] Jay, Meg. "The Downside of Cohabiting Before Marriage." The New York Times, The New York Times, 14 Apr. 2012, www.nytimes.com/2012/04/15/opinion/sunday/the-downside-of-cohabiting-before-marriage.html.

[39] Pearcey, Nancy. Love Thy Body: Answering Hard Questions about Life and Sexuality. Baker Books, 2019

[40] Pearcey, Nancy. Love Thy Body: Answering Hard Questions about Life and Sexuality. Baker Books, 2019

[41] Chumley, Cheryl K. "William Barr, Voice from the Wilderness: Religion 'at the Core of Our Country'." The Washington Times, The Washington Times, 29 Jan. 2020, www.washingtontimes.com/news/2020/jan/29/william-barr-voice-wilderness-religion-core-our-co/.

[42] Roberts, Michael. "Caldara: Denver Post Fired Me Because of Political Correctness." Westword, 4, 24 Jan. 2020, www.westword.com/news/denver-post-columnist-jon-caldara-i-was-fired-for-not-being-politically-correct-11614187.

[43] "State Officials Remove Several Books from Sex Ed Guidelines After Parent Protest." California Family Council, 15 May 2019, californiafamily.org/2019/state-officials-remove-several-books-from-sex-ed-guidelines-after-parent-protest/.

[44] DeMar, Gary. God and Government. American Vision Press, 2001

[45] http://fathers.com/statistics-and-research/the-consequences-of-fatherlessness/

[46] Gilkerson, Luke. "Updated Pornography Statistics." Covenant Eyes, 10 Apr. 2015, www.covenanteyes.com/2010/01/06/updated-pornography-statistics/.

[47] https://www.pastoralcareinc.com/statistics/

[48] Benner, David G. Surrender to Love: Discovering the Heart of Christian Spirituality. IVP Books, 2015.

[49] Mount Vernon.orge Education/ primary resources. George Washington Farewell Address 1796.

[50] "Carmen Alexe: People." Carmen Alexe Author, Foundation for Economic Education, 7 Aug. 2015, fee.org/people/carmen-alexe.

[51] "Nation (n.)." Index, www.etymonline.com/word/nation.

[52] Websters 1828 Dictionary

[53] DeMar, Gary. God and Government. American Vision Press, 2001

[54] DeMar, Gary. God and Government. American Vision Press, 2001

[55] Britannica. Constitutional Government.

[56] DeMar, Gary. God and Government. American Vision Press, 2001

57 Encyclopedia, Britannica. Life Expectancy
58 Wikipedia, Life Expectancy
59 Eleftheriou-Smith, Loulla-Mae. "7 Questions You're Too Embarrassed to Ask about the Magna Carta." The Independent, Independent Digital News and Media, 2 Feb. 2015, www.independent.co.uk/news/uk/magna-carta-what-is-it-and-why-is-it-still-important-today-10017258.html
60 The English Bill of Rights.
61 Hillsdale.edu Constitution 101. The Meaning and History of the Constitution. Natural Rights and the American Revolution, Thomas G. West.
62 The Declaration of Independence.
63 Hillsdale.edu, Constitution 101: The Meaning and History of the Constituion. Natural Rights and the American Revolution, Thomas G. West
64 The Declaration of Independence.
65 The Declaration of Independence.
6666 "George Washington, December 23, 1783, Resignation Address." The Library of Congress, www.loc.gov/resource/mgw3a.007/?sp=162&st=text.
67 Spalding, Matthew. "The Man Who Would Not Be King." The Heritage Foundation, www.heritage.org/commentary/the-man-who-would-not-be-king.
68 III, Edmin Meese, et al. "The Heritage Guide to The Constitution." Guide to the Constitution, www.heritage.org/constitution/#!/introessays/1/the-meaning-of-the-constitution.
69 "The Finger of God on the Constitutional Convention." WallBuilders, 4 Apr. 2017, wallbuilders.com/finger-god-constitutional-convention/.
70 "The Finger of God on the Constitutional Convention." WallBuilders, 4 Apr. 2017, wallbuilders.com/finger-god-constitutional-convention/.
71 Hillsdale.edu, Natural Rights and the American Revolution, Thomas G. West
72 "The Constitution." The White House, The United States Government, www.whitehouse.gov/about-the-white-house/the-constitution/.
73 Hillsdale.edu 2. Constitution 101: The Meaning and History of the Constitution. The Theory and Declaration of the Constitution Lecture, Larry P. Arnn.
74 Hamilton, Alexander, et al. The Federalist Papers Alexander Hamilton, James Madison, John Jay. Yale University Press, 2009.
75 Hillsdale.edu 2. Constitution 101: The Meaning and Theory of the Constitution. The Theory and Declaration of the Constitution Lecture, Larry P. Arnn.
76 Hamilton, Alexander, et al. The Federalist Papers Alexander Hamilton, James Madison, John Jay. Yale University Press, 2009.

77 III, Edmin Meese, et al. "The Heritage Guide to The Constitution." Guide to the Constitution, www.heritage.org/constitution/#!/introessays/1/the-meaning-of-the-constitution.

78 III, Edmin Meese, et al. "The Heritage Guide to The Constitution." Guide to the Constitution, www.heritage.org/constitution/#!/introessays/1/the-meaning-of-the-constitution.

79 Hillsdale.edu 2. Constitution 101: The Meaning and Theory of the Constituion. The Theory and Declaration of the Constitution Lecture, Larry P. Arnn

80 Hillsdale College. Online Courses. Constitution 101. The Meaning and the History of the Constitution. Lecturers noted. Dr. Larry P. Arrn., Dr.Ronald Pestritto and Charles and Lucia Shipley

81 "Lincoln on Thomas Jefferson." National Parks Service, U.S. Department of the Interior, www.nps.gov/liho/learn/historyculture/jefferson.htm.

82 Hillsdale.edu 3. Constitution 101, The Meaning and History of the Constitution. The Progressive Rejection of the Principles of the Declaration. Pestritto, Ronald

83 Hillsdale.edu 3. Constitution 101, The Meaning and History of the Constitution. The Progressive Rejection of the Principles of the Declaration. Pestritto, Ronald.

84 Hillsdale.edu. Constitution 101: The Meaning and History of the Constitution. The Progressive Rejection of the Founding and the rise of Bureaucratic Despotism. Ronald Pestritto and Charles and Lucia Shipley

85 Upham, David. "The Primacy of Property Rights and the American Founding: David Upham." FEE Freeman Article, Foundation for Economic Education, 1 Feb. 1998, fee.org/articles/the-primacy-of-property-rights-and-the-american-founding/.

86 Upham, David. "The Primacy of Property Rights and the American Founding: David Upham." FEE Freeman Article, Foundation for Economic Education, 1 Feb. 1998, fee.org/articles/the-primacy-of-property-rights-and-the-american-founding/.

87 A Defense of the Constitutions of the Government of the United States of America, 1787

88 James Madison Essay on Property, 1792

89 Thomas Jefferson, First Inaugural Address 1901

90 Upham, David. "The Primacy of Property Rights and the American Founding: David Upham." FEE Freeman Article, Foundation for Economic Education, 1 Feb. 1998, fee.org/articles/the-primacy-of-property-rights-and-the-american-founding/.

A Defense of the Constitutions of the Government of the United States of America, 1787

[91] "Carmen Alexe: People." Carmen Alexe Author, Foundation for Economic Education, 7 Aug. 2015, fee.org/people/carmen-alexe.
[92] Gordon, Thomas. "Why Socialism Often Leads to Tyranny: Thomas Gordon." FEE Freeman Article, Foundation for Economic Education, 3 Feb. 2020,
[93] Mount Vernon.org, Library. George Washington's Farewell Address
[94] Admin. "Howard Zinn on His Philosophy: Democratic Socialism." SACSIS.org.za, sacsis.org.za/s/story.php?s=890.
[95] Endorsement of Debunking Howard Zinn Exposing the fake history that turned a Generation against America.
[96] Vinton, Kate. "These 15 Billionaires Own America's News Media Companies." Forbes, Forbes Magazine, 2 June 2016, www.forbes.com/sites/katevinton/2016/06/01/these-15-billionaires-own-americas-news-media-companies/#4cbf2d64660a.
[97] Seminar with Warren Cole Smith. 2/8/2020 Chuck Colson Institute.
[98] Tash, Debra. "Project Veritas Insider Honored with Impact Award." Citizens Journal, 6 Dec. 2019, www.citizensjournal.us/project-veritas-insider-honored-with-impact-award/.
[99] United States Constitution." Wikipedia, Wikimedia Foundation, 1 June 2019, en.wikipedia.org/wiki/United States Constitution.
[100] "The Bill of Rights." Ushistory.org, Independence Hall Association, www.ushistory.org/us/18a.asp.

Evalyn Benton, Sam Benton
Contact us at Encounterprayer.org

My husband, Sam, and I live in Charlotte, N.C. where we have been praying for revival in our city over the last fifteen years.

We have been in pastoral ministry for thirty-five years. Sam and I are available to train, activate or support the prayer ministry within your community or church.

We are also available to conduct seminars on prayer, family ministry or to bring encouragement to your church through teaching and prophetic ministry.

Made in the USA
Columbia, SC
26 February 2020